HQ 784 .S45 I82 2010

Is childhood becoming too
sexualized?

DATE DUE

Demco, Inc. 38-293

At Issue

Is Childhood Becoming
Too Sexualized?

Other Books in the At Issue Series:

At Issue

Is Childhood Becoming Too Sexualized?

Olivia Ferguson and Hayley Mitchell Haugen,
Book Editors

GREENHAVEN PRESS
A part of Gale, Cengage Learning

GALE
CENGAGE Learning™

Detroit • New York • San Francisco • New Haven, Conn • Waterville, Maine • London

9\10

535494176

GALE
CENGAGE Learning™

Christine Nasso, *Publisher*
Elizabeth Des Chenes, *Managing Editor*

© 2010 Greenhaven Press, a part of Gale, Cengage Learning.

Gale and Greenhaven Press are registered trademarks used herein under license.

For more information, contact:
Greenhaven Press
27500 Drake Rd.
Farmington Hills, MI 48331-3535
Or you can visit our Internet site at gale.cengage.com

For product information and technology assistance, contact us at

Gale Customer Support, 1-800-877-4253
For permission to use material from this text or product, submit all requests online at
www.cengage.com/permissions

Further permissions questions can be e-mailed to permissionrequest@cengage.com

Articles in Greenhaven Press anthologies are often edited for length to meet page require-ments. In addition, original titles of these works are changed to clearly present the main thesis and to explicitly indicate the author's opinion. Every effort is made to ensure that Greenhaven Press accurately reflects the original intent of the authors. Every effort has been made to trace the owners of copyrighted material.

Cover image © Images.com/Corbis.

LIBRARY OF CONGRESS CATALOGING-IN-PUBLICATION DATA

Is childhood becoming too sexualized? / Olivia Ferguson and Hayley Mitchell Haugen, book editors.
     p. cm. -- (At issue)
   Includes bibliographical references and index.
   ISBN 978-0-7377-4884-0 (hbk.) -- ISBN 978-0-7377-4885-7 (pbk.)
   1. Children and sex--Juvenile literature. 2. Children--Sexual behavior--Juvenile literature. I. Ferguson, Olivia. II. Haugen, Hayley Mitchell, 1968-
   HQ784.S45I82 2010
   306.7083--dc22
                                                                2010013191

Printed in the United States of America
1 2 3 4 5 6 7 14 13 12 11 10

Contents

Introduction

According to the American Pregnancy Association, of the 6 million pregnancies every year throughout the United States, 468,988 babies are born to teenage mothers. Of the more than 15 million new cases of sexually transmitted diseases (STDs) each year, 3 million of these cases are among teenagers. As these statistics clearly suggest, many American teenagers are sexually active. How American society views this sexual activity, however, is contradictory. Sexually active boys are culturally considered to be acting out healthy and normal sexual urges, while sexually active girls are often culturally considered depraved.

Deborah L. Tolman writes of this double standard in her book, *Dilemmas of Desire: Teenage Girls Talk About Sexuality.* Here, she argues that American culture does not allow girls to have any kind of sexual subjectivity, meaning they are not allowed to see themselves as sexual beings. While boys are encouraged to explore their sexual impulses, girls frequently cannot act on their sexual desires without negative social repercussions.

"The possibility that girls might be interested in sexuality in their own right rather than as objects of boys' desire is met with resistance and discomfort," Tolman writes. This resistance is suggested by a culture of teen magazines, movies, television shows, and music videos, which Tolman claims, "continue to represent the belief that adolescent girls should be sexy for boys and not have their *own* sexual desire." Tolman questions this hypocritical stance and worries about the impact it has on both boys and girls.

One negative impact of ignoring sexual desire in girls is that it takes away their sexual agency—their power to make their own choices about sex. They may come to view themselves as only sexual commodities, as sexual objects to be admired and used by boys. Boys, in turn, are also encouraged to view girls as sexual objects. A frequent result of this kind of thinking about sex and desire is abuse. Tolman cites two studies that corroborate this idea. One study by the national Youth Risk Behavior Survey in 2000 found that 12.5 percent of girls in ninth through twelfth grades reported having been forced to have sexual intercourse. Another study in 2001 reported that one in five teenage girls experiences some form of dating or sexual violence during her high school years. Tolman believes that these statistics prove that American culture needs to rethink its stance on adolescent sexual desire. She argues, "If we not only accept but in fact expect adolescent boys to have strong sexual feelings they need to learn how to deal with, why don't we expect the same of girls?"

Many researchers believe that the answer to Tolman's question lies in the way that boys and girls are sexualized in American culture. Authors Diane E. Levin and Jean Kilbourne discuss the early sexualization of children in their book, *So Sexy So Soon: The New Sexualized Childhood and What Parents Can Do to Protect Their Kids.* Levin and Kilbourne worry about the "graphic messages about sex and sexiness in the media and popular culture," which bombard children from an early age. While they agree that children are sexual beings from birth and that sexual desire is a natural thing, they explain that the sexualization of children is different from healthy sexuality. In fact, the sexualization of children exploits children's sexuality.

The sexualization of children occurs when children internalize cultural messages about sexuality. From the popular, scantily clad Bratz dolls that young girls emulate, to the sexy thong underwear marketed to seven-year-olds, to the violent rap lyrics and racy music videos that encourage boys to act like pimps, Levin and Kilbourne argue that children are receiving very narrow definitions of sexuality. "A narrow definition of femininity and sexuality encourages girls to focus heavily on appearance and sex appeal," they write. "And boys who get a very narrow definition of masculinity that promotes insensitivity and macho behavior, are taught to judge girls based on how close they come to an artificial, impossible, and shallow ideal."

In addition to having a negative impact on children's understanding of gender, sexuality, and relationships, Levin and Kilbourne argue that the early sexualization of children can "contribute to pathological sexual behavior, including sexual abuse, pedophilia, and prostitution." The sexualization of children also encourages "dangerous attitudes" that make it "seem normal to look upon children as sex objects."

While most people thinking and writing about the topic of the sexualization of children tend to agree that the American media and consumer culture do have some effect on children, not everyone agrees on the causes of sexualization. Some researchers agree with Levin and Kilbourne that toys and clothing have a great impact in the matter of sexualization. Others focus almost entirely on the role of music, movies, television, and the Internet. Some writers blame Hollywood's young starlets for not being good role models to America's youth. Still, there are many others who feel that the contemporary panic over the sexualization of children is totally overdramatized.

Differing viewpoints on these and other topics are reflected in *At Issue: Is Childhood Becoming Too Sexualized?* Each viewpoint provides an enlightening look at many of the controversies inherent in the ongoing debate over the sexualization of children.

1

The Sexualization of Girls Is Harmful

AboutKidsHealth

AboutKidsHealth is an online resource and an initiative of the Hospital for Sick Children in Toronto, Canada. The site provides families with information about all areas of children's health and family life, in an easy to understand format.

Today's sex-saturated culture prevents healthy psychological development among girls. Cultural contributions to the sexualization of girls come from the media and marketing. Television shows and music videos frequently objectify women, and even Disney movies created for children contain sexy heroines. There are also interpersonal contributions to the sexualization of girls. Parents, teachers, and peers can all influence girls through gender typing and sexual harassment. Girls may even objectify themselves through their own choices about clothes and behavior. The sexualization of girls has far-reaching consequences. Girls may not only experience feelings of shame due to being sexualized, but they may also develop eating disorders, low self-esteem, and depression. To counteract the influence of sexualization, schools can implement media literacy programs and comprehensive sexual education. Families should talk with their children about the sexualized stereotypes they view on television, and girls themselves can organize groups to protest sexualization, develop critical perspectives, and lobby for social change.

Clothing stores sell thongs for seven- to 10-year-olds, some with slogans like "wink wink" or "eye candy." In child beauty pageants, girls as young as five wear fake teeth, makeup, and hair extensions, and are encouraged to flirt with the audience by batting their false-eyelash-laden eyes. The 2005 Victoria's Secret Fashion Show on prime-time television featured models made up to resemble young girls dressed in sexy lingerie. Magazines, television, and the Internet abound with images portraying girls and women as sexualized objects. There is growing evidence that this sex-saturated culture harms healthy psychological development among both boys and girls.

Sexualization is not to be confused with healthy sexuality, which is important for mental and physical health. Sexualization occurs when:

- a person's value comes only from his or her sexual appeal or behaviour

- a person is held to a standard that equates physical attractiveness with being sexy

- a person is sexually objectified—made into a thing for others' sexual use

- sexuality is inappropriately imposed upon a person

Professionals and parents have been growing more aware and concerned about the sexualization of girls and its consequences. In response to this concern, the American Psychological Association established the Task Force on the Sexualization of Girls, consisting of six psychologists and a member of the public, in February 2005. More than two dozen other psychologists contributed to the report through comments and reviews.

The task force's report was recently published by the American Psychological Association. In it, the authors define sexualization, describe how it takes place, describe its effects on girls and society as a whole, and recommend positive alternatives. Their findings and recommendations have implications for families, schools, organizations, and professionals that work with children and youth and government policies.

Cultural Contributions to the Sexualization of Girls

Media. The average child views over six hours of media per day. Among prime-time television shows popular with children and adolescents, 12% of sexual comments involved sexual objectification, the vast majority directed toward women. Other research showed that 23% of sexual behaviours observed on prime-time programs involved leering, ogling, or catcalling at female characters. Many comments concerned body parts or nudity, and 85% of the comments came from men. Up to 81% of music videos contain sexual imagery, the majority of which sexually objectifies women by presenting them in revealing clothing, as decorative sexual objects, dancing sexually, or in ways that emphasize body parts or sexual readiness.

Similar patterns of sexualization and objectification are present in song lyrics, movies, and magazines. Some researchers have observed that even among animated Disney movies, contemporary heroines (the Little Mermaid, Pocahontas) are "sexier" than some of the historical characters (Snow White, Cinderella).

"Sexy" clothing such as thongs and lingerie is now manufactured in children's sizes.

In sports media and other media, female athletes are more likely to be portrayed as sexual objects than male athletes. Eight female Olympic athletes were featured in the September 2004 issue of *Playboy*.

Products. Dolls designed for four- to eight-year-old girls, such as the Bratz or Trollz dolls, are clad in sexualized clothing such as miniskirts, fishnet stockings, and feather boas, with accessories such as "magical belly gems." "Sexy" clothing such as thongs and lingerie is now manufactured in children's sizes and marketed to tweens, defined by some stores as girls seven and up. The cosmetics industry markets perfumes, lip glosses, and other toiletries to young girls.

Interpersonal Contributions

Parents. Fathers' attitudes are particularly powerful influences on gender typing and whether or not children conform to this typing. Current culture stresses the physical attractiveness of thinness. The "thin ideal" is thus related to the sexualization of girls, and is often reinforced in mother-daughter interactions.

There is also a trend for an increase in parents condoning plastic surgery for their daughters. Since 2000, the number of invasive cosmetic surgeries performed in the United States on teens 18 or under has increased 15%, to 77,000.

Teachers. Research has shown that teachers encourage girls to play "dress up" more than boys. This type of play often involves vamping and looking in mirrors. Some work has shown that teachers have negative attitudes toward girls whose bodies do not conform to the thin ideal.

Peers. Girls are marked by boys as sexual at an early age, independent of the girls' behaviour. Girls enforce conformity with ideals of thinness and sexiness. Negative sexualization of teen girls by peers, for example by characterizing them as "sluts," is used as a form of social aggression among peers. Popularity of girls is based in part on physical attractiveness and a precocious interest in boys.

Sexual harassment perpetrated by boys and men in schools and in the workplace is a common form of social aggression.

Girls as young as 10 experience sexual harassment at school. Pubertal development leads to increased sexual harassing comments for girls, in turn promoting increased feelings of shame about their bodies. Sexual abuse, the most damaging form of sexual harassment, has a lifetime prevalence rate for women of between 15% and 20%.

Self-objectification. Girls contribute to their own sexualization through their choice of clothes and behaviour. This arises out of a desire for social advantage, for example popularity, and out of fear of social rejection if they do not make these types of choices. The focus on physical attractiveness as a method of self-improvement and social success is more prevalent in the last 20 years than previously.

The authors of the report make clear that girls do not make these choices independently; they are bound up in the cultural and interpersonal influences that surround them.

Consequences of the Sexualization of Girls

The sexualization of girls and women has far-reaching consequences. At the individual level, there are negative effects on cognitive and physical functioning and mental health. Negative consequences are also experienced by women, boys, men, and society at large.

It is not surprising that feelings of inadequacy and shame are widespread.

Sexualization Affects Girls

Objectification theory is a psychological theory that directly explains the mechanism by which sexualization influences the well-being of girls and women. It combines socialization, sociocultural, cognitive, and psychoanalytic approaches, arguing that girls' observations of the world lead to self-objectification and self-sexualization. The process involves adopting a third-person perspective, assessing and controlling the sexual desirability of one's own body to others in terms of culturally given standards of attractiveness, rather than on the basis of one's own desires, health, competence, or achievements. Forces leading to the sexualization of girls influence their development in particularly vulnerable periods. Cultural messages about sexuality impinge on children too young to cope with them and influence identity formation during early adolescence, contributing to a loss in self-esteem during this critical period of identity development.

The consequences of this self-objectification are far-reaching, disrupting cognitive and physical functioning. The authors describe one striking study in which college students were asked to try on and evaluate either a swimsuit or a sweater. While waiting wearing the swimsuit or the sweater, they completed a math test. Girls wearing a swimsuit scored significantly worse than those wearing a sweater. No such effect was present for boys. The implication is that attention to physical appearance leaves fewer cognitive resources to complete other tasks.

The constant monitoring of appearance leads to feelings of shame. Feelings of shame arise from a perception that one has failed to meet cultural standards of conduct. Few girls meet the dominant cultural standard for a slender, sexy appearance, so it is not surprising that feelings of inadequacy and shame are widespread. Studies have also demonstrated that exposure to idealized models of sexual attractiveness in media such as fashion magazines leads to body dissatisfaction among girls. In extreme cases, body image dissatisfaction leads teenage girls to undergo plastic surgery procedures such as breast implants and liposuction for reduction of fat in the hips, belly, and thighs. It also contributes to the success of the cosmetics and beauty products industry. In the US [United States], girls between the ages of 12 and 19 spent $8 billion on these products and services.

Three of the most common mental health problems of girls and women, eating disorders, low self-esteem, and depression, have been linked to sexualization. The incidence of anorexia nervosa in girls 10 to 19 over the last 50 years has tracked changes in fashion, with the ideal of a thin body type preceding the highest incidences of anorexia nervosa. A number of studies have demonstrated the links between media exposure to idealized women and depression and reduced self-esteem.

Dr. Gail McVey, scientist and psychologist at the Hospital for Sick Children, has observed through her research that girls as young as 10 are resorting to extreme weight loss techniques in attempts to mimic the bodies of runway models. In addition to the media, girls face additional pressures such as appearance-based teasing, peer pressure to conform to the thin ideal of beauty, and sexual harassment. Girls learn through the process of socialization to base their self-worth on their appearance.

Healthy sexual development is also disrupted by sexual objectification. Evidence shows that exposure to and identification with media portrayals of women is associated with more negative attitudes toward breastfeeding and the functional aspects of one's own body. Media exposure also influences perceptions of sexual experience, including virginity and first sexual experiences. In one study, the most powerful predictor of love relationships among undergraduate women was amount of exposure to MTV. . . .

Counteracting the Influence of Sexualization

The report of the task force concludes with a section describing positive programs and approaches to counter sexualization and a series of recommendations. Three broad domains of activities are described that can take place in schools, within the family, and through working directly with girls and girls' groups.

Schools can implement media literacy programs and comprehensive sexual education; focus activity on physical activity and athletics that stress action, agency, and competence; encourage participation in extracurricular programs such as music, drama, and games that stress development of a talent or skill; and provide alternatives to activities that emphasize beauty, thinness, and sex appeal.

A supportive relationship between dads and daughters . . . can help boost self-esteem in girls.

In the home, parents can watch television with their children and engage in discussions of the portrayals of women, stereotyped relationships, and aggression. Organized religion or other forms of ethical instruction, a strong sense of spirituality, or the practice of meditation often originate with the family and can serve to contract effects of media representations and other negative social forces. Parents and families can become activists by, for example, opposing media sexualization of girls through grassroots techniques such as letter-writing campaigns. . . .

Dr. McVey's research has demonstrated that a supportive relationship between dads and daughters, particularly during the early adolescent years, can help boost self-esteem in girls and help prevent the development of body image dissatisfaction. . . .

Alternative media such as online magazines or Web logs (blogs) can provide a forum to help girls critically examine the sexualizing images and media portrayals of girls and women. Girls can organize as groups to protest sexualization, develop critical perspectives, and lobby for social change in the public sphere.

2

Sexualization of Girls Teaches Boys to Be Sexually Violent

Rachel Bell

Rachel Bell is a regular commentator for the Independent, *a British daily newspaper founded in 1986.*

The sexualization of girls teaches boys to be sexually violent. Rape is at crisis levels, and it is ordinary boys and men who commit rape and other violence against women. The normalization of sex and pornography makes it acceptable for boys to see women as sex objects, and boys are pressured by their peers to buy into this view of women to prove their own masculinity. The effect of eroticizing sexual harassment and violence against women, however, is that it not only prevents boys from relating to girls, it also prevents them from truly knowing their own humanity.

It's official: Sexualisation harms girls. Of course it does. It harms all of us. It doesn't just make girls ill, it harms boys too, teaching them to be sexually violent.

The American Psychological Association's findings—that the portrayal of girls and young women as sex objects harms girls' mental and physical health—should be addressed at the root cause: the media. Powerful and profit driven, they are left to self-regulate with their own voluntary codes. Not only is this not working, it's harming society. The government needs to introduce responsible media regulation, in which social responsibility and harm are not compromised for free speech. Only then will we see diverse representations of females in positive roles.

As a society, we should be extremely worried. The saturation of sexualised images of females is leading to body hatred, eating disorders, low self-esteem, depression, high rates of teen pregnancy and unhealthy sexual development in our girl children. It also leads to impaired cognitive performance. In short, if we tell girls that looking "hot" is the only way to be validated, rather than encouraging them to be active players in the world, they underperform at everything else.

But the consequences of sexualising girls are far more devastating than this. Rape is at crisis levels, and one in three women will be a victim of stalking, sexual harassment or sexual violence in her lifetime.

Only 8 percent of rapes are stranger rapes.

Alcohol Does Not Rape Girls

But who are the mysterious perpetrators of these crimes? Much of the media, the justice system and one-third of the public seem to think alcohol is raping girls. That by getting drunk, dressing sexy and flirting, girls and women are responsible for the horrific violence committed against them.

Only 8 percent of rapes are stranger rapes. It is ordinary boys and men who are committing these sexually violent crimes against girls and women. It is appalling that when another rape or sexually violent crime is reported on the news—so ubiquitous it is unremarkable—it is never followed by a report asking: "Why are boys and men sexually abusing and raping girls and women? Where do they learn to film this abuse on their mobiles? Where do boys and men learn that having power over women and being violent is an acceptable way to be a man?" Instead, the onus is on girls and women to curb their behaviour and lives.

The sexualisation of girls and the normalisation of the sex and porn [pornography] industries have made it increasingly acceptable and "fun" for women to be viewed as sex objects, and for men to view women as sexual commodities. To speak out against this trend is framed as "anti-fun" and "anti-sex". The pressure group OBJECT has documented how men's "lifestyle" magazines and lad mags do not merely objectify women, they trivialise trafficking, sex tourism and prostitution. The number of young British men using prostitutes has doubled in a decade to one in 10 in 2000.

The charity the Lilith Project has found that the increasingly mainstream pole- and lap-dancing and porn industries are careful to hide their links with prostitution, trafficking and sexual violence. A five-year-old boy can buy a lad mag and learn that women are only sex objects and he has entitlements to their bodies. If he logs on to *Zoo* magazine's Web site, he can watch videos of girls stripping and lap-dancing, one set up as if the woman is being stalked and secretly filmed in her bedroom while she strips, another of a "ridiculously hot" girl being so frightened, she is screaming and crying uncontrollably in a ball. This is not just about sexualisation. Sexual harassment is being eroticised.

The absence of positive role models in boys' immediate lives is showing.

Boys Are Under Pressure to Be Masculine

The sexualisation of girls exploits girls and boys. All children and young people are under immense pressure to accept it. Boys who are not enthusiastic about it, or speak out against it, run the risk of being ignored or ridiculed, of being labelled "gay", "unmanly", or not liking sex. Boys and young men are under pressure to act out masculinity in which power and control over women, and men, is normal, in which violence is normal.

The absence of positive role models in boys' immediate lives is showing. If the adult men around them do not challenge sexism and traditional masculine behaviours, boys won't either. And with absent fathers, boys are left with celebrities and sports heroes to look up to. Music videos largely follow a template of an individual man possessing a group of sexualised women, gangsta rappers promote sexist and violent notions of masculinity, many young footballers and other sportsmen behave like playboys, enjoy group sex, get away with rape and keep their "hero" status.

Damian Carnell who works to prevent anti-gender violence, says: "From boyhood, men read into the messages that we see around us, from men's institutionalised superiority over women, and privileges of being male, to negative stereotypes of girls and women. It's no wonder that 35 percent of boys aged 11–16 believe it is justified to abuse women."

The sexualisation of girls is not just shattering the lives of girls and women, it is preventing boys and young men from relating to girls and women as complex human beings with so much to offer them. It is preventing boys from forming healthy friendships and working relationships with girls and women. Instead, it is nurturing potentially violent abusers, rapists and johns [clients of prostitutes]. Ultimately, it means boys are not free to be themselves, to know their own humanity.

3

The Sexualization of Children Socializes Boys to Become Sexual Predators

Carol Platt Liebau, as told to Kathryn Jean Lopez

Kathryn Jean Lopez is editor of National Review Online *and a conservative columnist.*

The current culture glorifies sex and portrays mainstream images of sexualized young girls. In a society where "slut" has become an acceptable term of affection among girlfriends, boys are conditioned to see girls as sex objects. Lopez argues that when girls are encouraged to play a sexualized role, boys live up to the expected sexually vulgar and predator image.

Boldly, Carol Platt Liebau recently wrote a book about sex in America called *Prude[: How the Sex-Obsessed Culture Damages Girls (and America Too!)]*. To mark Valentine's Day, *National Review Online* editor Kathryn Jean Lopez asked Liebau about her book and our oversexed culture.

KATHRYN JEAN LOPEZ: Isn't declaring yourself a "Prude" a surefire way to never get a heart-shaped diamond on Valentine's Day?

CAROL PLATT LIEBAU: Well, it certainly isn't a recipe for romance! Our culture understands a "prude" to be someone who is "sexually conservative and no fun"—as Columbia University's online health counselor defined the word in re-

Kathryn Jean Lopez, "Sex in High School," *National Review Online*, February 14, 2008. Copyright © 2008 by National Review, Inc., 215 Lexington Avenue, New York, NY 10016. Reproduced by permission.

sponse to a question from a self-described "thirteen-year-old clueless girl." Who could blame a guy for being a little leery of someone who describes herself that way?

But as I point out in the book, the word "prude" derives from the old French "*prude femme,*" meaning "a good or virtuous woman." It's revealing that, these days, the term "slut" has become a widely accepted, affection term of familiarity among girlfriends, but being labeled a "prude" is nothing short of a social disaster.

Cultural Influences

LOPEZ: How is popular culture letting girls down? Is it doing the same to boys?

LIEBAU: America's popular culture has been letting girls down by teaching them, over and over, that the most important attribute they can have is "sexiness"—that it's more noteworthy than character, intelligence, or talent. "Sexy" has become the ultimate accolade, which is why everything from hair mousse to shades of lipstick to chefs to cameras are touted as being sexy.

Boys live up (or down) to the standards girls set for them.

When sexiness is the standard for what's deemed to be interesting and important, then of course you're going to see more girls doing everything from wearing revealing clothes to engaging in over-the-top sexual behaviors.

All of this has a spillover effect on boys, of course. When girls are encouraged to be coarse, there's a coarsening effect on boys, too, because boys live up (or down) to the standards girls set for them. Certainly, when girls behave in vulgar or crass ways, it erodes boys' innate desire to cherish, respect and protect them—which has always been one of the marks of a civilized society. What's more, bad behavior by girls enables and normalizes bad behavior on the boys' parts, so there ends up being more of it all around.

LOPEZ: You also point out that "young women in America have never had it better." So why whine about the culture when there's plenty good about it?

LIEBAU: "Whining"?! I hope not! Certainly, as I point out in *Prude*, by a whole host of measures—including school attendance and academics—girls are routinely outperforming boys, and writers like Christina Hoff Sommers have explained brilliantly why young men need our concern and attention in the areas where they're falling short.

Sexual activity devoid of emotion or commitment is the goal—and the hallmark of true female liberation.

Given how far, how fast girls have come, it becomes easy to dismiss the impact that the aggressive sexualizing of American culture has had on them. But it's important to remember that many girls can grow up to experience great professional or economic success and still suffer deep and long-lasting physical, emotional, psychological, and spiritual damage from having given too much, too soon.

"Empowerment" of Sex

LOPEZ: What is do-me feminism? And doom-me? Have feminists doomed American women?

LIEBAU: American women aren't victims—and feminists don't have the power to "doom" them without their own complicity. Nonetheless, pernicious attitudes with their genesis in radical feminism have infiltrated popular culture to a startling degree. Chief among them is the concept of "do-me feminism," which is the idea that somehow it's "empowering" for girls to act like the worst kinds of men when it comes to sex.

In this formulation, sexual activity devoid of emotion or commitment is the goal—and the hallmark of true female liberation.

The problem is that "do-me feminism" sets girls up for failure when it comes to their dealings with the opposite sex. As long as girls are innately more invested in relationships and emotions than boys are (as studies—and common sense—indicate), they will be at a grave disadvantage in a sexual landscape where optional, emotion-free, commitment-less sex is deemed the ultimate in "coolness" and liberation.

Ironically, do-me feminism has made it more difficult for girls to obtain the attention, affection, and connection they want from boys, even as its influence has made it harder for them to refuse what many boys want—sexual activity. By convincing girls that it somehow makes sense for them to offer their bodies quickly and easily, do-me feminism has essentially persuaded them to surrender their most effective means for securing the kind of male attention that they most desire.

As I argue in *Prude*, the whole concept of "do-me feminism" has done women a terrible disservice. Although they are—and certainly should be—considered equal before the law and in the eyes of the culture, men and women simply aren't the same. Girls are being led to believe they're in control when it comes to sexual relationships. In truth, however, they're living in a profoundly anti-feminist landscape where girls compete for attention on the basis of how much they are sexually willing to do for boys.

LOPEZ: What's the alternative? Are there solid pop culture models?

LIEBAU: Dr. Drew Pinsky, one of the experts who spoke to me, pointed out that that solid pop culture models for girls are few and far between. Instead, he advised, girls are often better off finding someone in their own lives—whether it's a mother, a big sister, a teacher—who's worth looking up to and emulating.

LOPEZ: Is teen pregnancy still a problem? Is Jamie Lynn Spears?

LIEBAU: Any parent criticizes Jamie Lynn Spears at her peril—who knows what her own children will do? But there's no doubt that her much-publicized pregnancy is just another example of the mainstreaming of the kind of sexual decision making that has an unfortunate impact not just on young women individually, but on a society collectively.

When it comes to teen pregnancy generally, rates rise and fall. Too often, it seems, we're willing to take pregnancy rates as a proxy for healthy or positive trends generally when it comes to teen sexuality. Part of my point in *Prude* was to try to demonstrate that girls can have sex and escape either an unwanted pregnancy or an STD [sexually transmitted disease]—but promiscuous sexual behavior *still* isn't a good idea for a whole host of reasons.

Sexual Integrity

LOPEZ: You write about Best Friends, PALS, and other programs—how prevalent are these abstinence-based programs and what is their secret?

It's discouraging to live in a world where porn stars publish best-selling autobiographies and pole dancing is touted as a new, mainstream form of aerobic exercise.

LIEBAU: Best Friends, PALS, and some of the other programs I discuss in my book aren't as prevalent as they need to be. A lot of the time, "abstinence" programs take a purely negative physical and/or economic approach to persuading young people to wait—in other words, "don't have sex or you could become pregnant or contract an STD, be unable to go to college," etc. The most effective programs are those, like Best Friends and PALS, that offer young people something both deeper and more transcendent—programs that teach sexual integrity as just one more component of good character overall.

LOPEZ: Are you optimistic about culture?

LIEBAU: Absolutely! Of course, that doesn't mean it's easy to figure out how to restore the notion of sexual innocence to girlhood. It's discouraging to live in a world where porn stars publish best-selling autobiographies and pole dancing is touted as a new, mainstream form of aerobic exercise. The fact that someone at a Florida Hooters thought, even for a minute, that it would be a good idea to hold a "Little Miss Hooters" contest for girls five years old and under—competitors to be dressed in orange spandex shorts and clingy "Hooters" t-shirts—boggles the mind.

Change for the better can and will come, but only when a critical mass of Americans decides that the tangible and intangible costs imposed by gratuitous sex in the public square are unacceptably high—and that it's more important to protect young peoples' innocence than it is to exercise the "right" to be exposed in public to titillating words and images.

This isn't about controlling what people do in the privacy of their own homes—that isn't anyone's business. Rather, it's about trying to restore some sanity to the public space and the popular culture that all of us share.

4

American Culture Rewards Girls for Eroticism

Lawrence Downes

Lawrence Downes is a member of the editorial board of the New York Times. *He writes opinion pieces on suburban issues for the Westchester, Long Island, and City sections of the paper.*

Girls as young as middle school age are being encouraged both by American culture and their parents to become eroticized. They wiggle and gyrate for applause at school talent shows, and at school dances, the pelvic thrusting that is being passed off as dancing is more a kind of simulated intercourse. While some parents may argue these behaviors are healthy fun, they are expressions of sexuality that should not go unchecked. Young girls should not be encouraged to act like little adults. Qualities other than sexual allure should be stressed for building personal power and self-esteem.

It's hard to write this without sounding like a prig. But it's just as hard to erase the images that planted the idea for this essay, so here goes. The scene is a middle school auditorium, where girls in teams of three or four are bopping to pop songs at a student talent show. Not bopping, actually, but doing elaborately choreographed re-creations of music videos, in tiny skirts or tight shorts, with bare bellies, rouged cheeks and glittery eyes.

They writhe and strut, shake their bottoms, splay their legs, thrust their chests out and in and out again. Some straddle empty chairs, like lap dancers without laps. They don't smile much. Their faces are locked from grim exertion, from all that leaping up and lying down without poles to hold onto. "Don't stop don't stop," sings Janet Jackson, all whispery. "Jerk it like you're making it choke. . . . Ohh. I'm so stimulated. Feel so X-rated." The girls spend a lot of time lying on the floor. They are in the sixth, seventh and eighth grades.

As each routine ends, parents and siblings cheer, whistle and applaud. I just sit there, not fully comprehending. It's my first suburban Long Island middle school talent show. I'm with my daughter, who is 10 and hadn't warned me. I'm not sure what I had expected, but it wasn't this. It was something different. Something younger. Something that didn't make the girls look so . . . one-dimensional.

Eroticism in popular culture is a 24-hour, all-you-can-eat buffet.

It would be easy to chalk it up to adolescent rebellion, an ancient and necessary phenomenon, except these girls were barely adolescents and they had nothing to rebel against. This was an official function at a public school, a milieu that in another time or universe might have seen children singing folk ballads, say, or reciting the Gettysburg Address.

Parents Encourage Eroticism

It is news to no one, not even me, that eroticism in popular culture is a 24-hour, all-you-can-eat buffet, and that many children in their early teens are filling up. The latest debate centers on whether simulated intercourse is an appropriate dance style for the high school gym.

What surprised me, though, was how completely parents of even younger girls seem to have gotten in step with society's march toward eroticized adolescence—either willingly or through abject surrender. And if parents give up, what can a school do? A teacher at the middle school later told me she had stopped chaperoning dances because she was put off by the boy-girl pelvic thrusting and had no way to stop it—the children wouldn't listen to her and she had no authority to send anyone home. She guessed that if the school had tried to ban the sexy talent show routines, parents would have been the first to complain, having shelled out for costumes and private dance lessons for their Little Miss Sunshines.

I'm sure that many parents see these routines as healthy fun, an exercise in self-esteem harmlessly heightened by glitter makeup and teeny skirts. Our girls are bratz, not slutz, they would argue, comfortable in the existence of a distinction.

There is no reason adulthood should be a low plateau we all clamber onto around age 10.

But my parental brain rebels. Suburban parents dote on and hover over their children, micromanaging their appointments and shielding them in helmets, kneepads and thick layers of SUV [sport-utility vehicle] steel. But they allow the culture of boy-toy sexuality to bore unchecked into their little ones' ears and eyeballs, displacing their nimble and growing brains and impoverishing the sense of wider possibilities in life.

There is no reason adulthood should be a low plateau we all clamber onto around age 10. And it's a cramped vision of girlhood that enshrines sexual allure as the best or only form of power and esteem. It's as if there were now Three Ages of Woman: first Mary-Kate, then Britney, then Courtney. Boys don't seem to have such constricted horizons. They wouldn't stand for it—much less waggle their butts and roll around for applause on the floor of a school auditorium.

5

The Physical Aggression Encouraged in Boys Is a Form of Sexualization

Elizabeth Anne Wood

Elizabeth Anne Wood is a self-described sex radical and feminist sociologist. She writes the blog Sex in the Public Square, through which she shares her belief that no kind of consensual sex or gender identity should be stigmatized. Wood studies sex work, sexual identity, and the commoditization of sex and love in the United States. She teaches sociology at Nassau Community College in New York.

Lawrence Downes, a contributor to the New York Times, *claims that boys would never allow themselves to be objectified in the way he sees young girls being eroticized for applause at their school talent shows. Boys, however, are constantly reducing themselves to spectacle through their participation in sports, especially football. Football rewards boys for their physicality and their aggressive behavior, yet no one is outraged by this lauding of their masculinity. American culture values aggression in boys, but aggression can lead to negative things, such as abusiveness and bullying. Sexuality, on the other hand, can connote more positive things, such as pleasure and communication. Society privileges boys' performance of gender, yet criticizes girls for it and tries to limit their personal expression.*

What follows is a slightly revised version of a blog post published on Sex in the Public Square on December 29, 2006. Extra-

Elizabeth Anne Wood, "'Middle School Girls Gone Wild' . . . Really? I Think the Boys Are Wilder!" Sex in the Public Square Blog, December 29, 2006. Reproduced by permission.

neous material relevant to the blog at the time but not relevant here has been removed. A few passages have been refined. Otherwise, it remains as originally published. A follow-up post was published on January 5, 2007. Sex in the Public Square later moved to a new Web address: http://sexinthepublicsquare.org

This morning a *New York Times* piece really irritated me. This piece, written by Lawrence Downes, the father of a middle school girl, begins with the words "It's hard to write this without sounding like a prig" and ends with the declaration, "Boys don't seem to have such constricted horizons. They wouldn't stand for it—much less waggle their butts and roll around for applause on the floor of a school auditorium."

Without reading the piece you can pretty much imagine its contents: middle-aged parent of middle school child sits in middle school auditorium watching a talent show which, predictably, falls pretty short on imagination and talent. The girls writhe around like stripper-wanna-bes to sexually explicit Janet Jackson lyrics (yes, what would outrage at mass media sexualization of girls [be] without a swipe at Janet Jackson). The boys, somehow, never appear on stage. Or if they do, we never learn what their acts consist of. We are just told that they would never "waggle their butts and roll around for applause on the floor." Hmm. Really?

Why are we not outraged at the valuing of young boys' bodies and the lauding of their masculinity in organized competitive sports like football?

It was not Downes's objections to the sexualized performance of the 6th, 7th, and 8th grade girls that angered me, though I would remind him that this is hardly a new phenomenon, and that way back in the 80s—good god 20 years ago—when I was in middle school, girls were prancing around imitating Madonna, Cindy Lauper and, yes, Janet Jackson.

What angered me was his assertion that boys would never let themselves be so reduced to this kind of spectacle, yet he neglects to describe the boys' performances at all.

While I can't reflect at all on the boys at the talent show because they were deemed unremarkable, there is no question in my mind that boys are constantly reducing themselves to such spectacle. And that they are rewarded for doing so. Perhaps theirs is not an overtly sexualized spectacle, but a spectacle that rewards them for their physicality, their bodies, their gender performance, and their writhing. A spectacle that places them in danger and that lauds their violent or at the very least aggressive behavior. A spectacle that reduces their gender-role options rather than expanding them. And parents of boys are generally not appalled. No, in fact, this is seen as so commonplace that it is not worth even mentioning. No, beyond that, it is seen as so spectacular, so wonderful, that we organize leagues and teams and television channels and billion-dollar advertising campaigns around it. It is football.

Why are we not outraged at the valuing of young boys' bodies and the lauding of their masculinity in organized competitive sports like football?

American Culture Values Aggression in Boys

We are not angry about that because we believe that such activities prepare boys to be men. In fact, we so believe that the skills and capacities learned in sports are beneficial that we encourage girls to get involved too. Certainly capacities for teamwork and cooperation and the discipline of training are all very important. But those can be generated in a number of ways that are less aggressive than, say, football, a sport on which colleges and universities depend for money, which exploits the bodies of young men and subjects them to debilitating injury, (see recent *New York Times* coverage of brain injury and professional football), but for which we celebrate them as participants.

We are not angry because we *value* aggression in boys. We see it as a sign of their masculinity. Apparently we don't feel as strongly about valuing sexuality in girls. And that's unfortunate, really. Think about it: Aggression is rarely a positive attribute. In fact, boys and men end up struggling with their aggression in relationships with others. Aggression: fighting, abusiveness, intimidation, bullying. Sexuality, on the other hand, is a potential source of pleasure, playfulness, intimacy, connection, communication. I don't mean to suggest that it is *always* associated with these things, but the potential is always there within sexual experience to lead to these things. This is not true of aggression. It is hard to imagine aggression leading to anything particularly positive.

I'm angry because we privilege boys for their physical performances of gender even when those performances depend on aggression and even violence, yet we criticize girls for their physical performances of gender, especially when those involve overt displays of sexuality. In fact, I'm going to go out on a limb here and suggest that one of the reasons we are so fearful about our girls displaying their sexuality is because we fear what might happen to them at the hands of aggressive, out-of-control boys! Yet somehow it seems better to limit the girls' personal expression than try to change the culture of violent masculinity.

It is hard to imagine aggression leading to anything particularly positive.

I hope Mr. Downes rethinks his talent show experience. What were the boys' performances reflecting? It is interesting that they were not described at all. I suppose they were completely unremarkable—normative in fact. Perhaps this is another reflection of masculinity as standard. And what about all those *other* instances where boys are rewarded for a very narrow, very physical, very exploitive, dangerous set of performances? If Mr. Downes is serious about his concern for gender equality, as he seems to be by his closing declaration, I hope he reexamines his feelings about the performances of these middle school girls in light of a new examination of middle school boys' activities. I think he might find the range to be equally narrow, and the outcome to be much worse.

6

Sexualization of Children Is Not the Problem It Is Reported to Be

Kerry Howley

Kerry Howley is a senior editor at Reason *magazine. Her writing has also appeared in the* New York Times, *the* Los Angeles Times, Reader's Digest, *and elsewhere. She appears regularly as a commentator on the Fox News Channel.*

The American Psychological Association (APA) warns in a report that American teens are over-sexualized and at risk in society now more than ever before. This report, however, is lacking in statistical evidence to back up its findings and relies heavily on slippery slope anecdotes. It does not, for example, address whether teens choose provocative clothing to impress men or to fit in with their peers. The APA also does not address the fact that girls are more powerful in American society than ever before. Teen pregnancy is down, and college enrollment for girls is up. Sexual victimization rates have also fallen, suggesting that the so-called sexualization of girls in American culture has not resulted in increased violence against them. Until researchers can more specifically verify a connection between teen girls' fashion choices and violence, and between their purported over-sexualization and depression or low self-esteem, they should keep their social disapproval to themselves.

Just how far along the slick slope of cultural decline have we fallen? While you've been reading the Superficial [a celebrity gossip Web site] and playing Hot or Not [a Web site that allows users to rate the attractiveness of photos], the American Psychological Association's [APA's] Task Force on the Sexualization of Girls has been hard at work chronicling our sexed up, dumbed down culture. Liberals and conservatives alike are convinced, it seems, that a toxic mix of toys, music, and media is turning tweens [preteens] into tarts.

It's all here, in 72 titillating pages—the Kid Rock lyrics (So blow me bitch I don't rock for cancer/I rock for the cash and the topless dancers), the characterization of the Internet as a conduit for porn [pornography], the descent of the model Disney heroine from modest maiden (Snow White) to "sexy" strumpet (the Little Mermaid.) They're about two years behind the *Us Weekly* crowd—Christina Aguilera, Britney Spears . . . and Paris Hilton all figure prominently—but it hardly matters. The cast here is changeable, the message eminently recyclable: American teens are at risk like never before.

Well, there is a slight innovation at play in the APA's retelling of good girls gone bad. We've apparently moved beyond the age of the tarted up tween and into the era of the prostitot, the epoch of the kinderwhore. The hallowed thong, "an item of clothing based on what a stripper might wear," now comes in kid sizes. "Pudgy, cuddly, and asexual troll dolls" have been traded for "Trollz [dolls]," apparently highly gendered. Even the American Girl dolls, who might as well come packaged with promise rings on their porcelain figures, are not immune. "American Girl's recent co-branding with Bath & Body Works," we learn, "may lead to product tie-ins that will encourage girls to develop a precocious body consciousness and one associated with narrowly sexual attractiveness." And let's not even get started on Bratz [dolls].

The report is short on numbers, heavy on anecdote. But it's easy to be persuaded that eight-year-olds are dressing more like tweens, tweens more like teens, and teens more like 20-somethings. Which means—what exactly? Kids ape their older peers, and they've never had more access to images of underdressed celebutants. A sixth grader in a short skirt could well be a sign of a sexually dysfunctional society, a pie-eyed Paris in the making. Or she could simply suggest that 11-year-olds pick an outfit the same way they long have, hoping to find acceptance within a social group and signal mastery over a shared culture. Fashion can suggest sexual availability, or it can imply inclusion. Are they dressing for men, or for one another?

We've apparently moved beyond the age of the tarted up tween and into the era of the prostitot, the epoch of the kinderwhore.

It's not a question the APA bothers to address. The authors present the escalating Hilton/thong/Bratz situation beside a litany of alarming pathologies that sexualization might conceivably provoke, from eating disorders to depression to low self-esteem to addiction. There is no suggestion that some girls are more vulnerable to these problems than others; the weight of an underdressed Lindsay Lohan burdens all of us equally. The report then moves seamlessly from low self-esteem to violent, predatory behavior. Sex abuse "is an extreme form of sexualization," just a few steps away from those Trollz on the alleged sex continuum.

Girls Are More Powerful than Ever

Again, the report is a designated stat-free zone, but numbers on the state of girlhood are dramatic enough to be worth repeating. The Guttmacher Institute reports that the teen pregnancy rate in 2002, the latest year available, was at its lowest level in 30 years. Between 1998 and 2002, the teenage abortion rate dropped 50 percent. Women are 56 percent of college enrollees. Girls have made such strides that conservatives in search of a cause (and eager to blame feminists) have dubbed the reverse gender gap the "War on Boys." And while those celebrities the girls are slavishly aping cycle in and out of rehab, teen drug and alcohol use are both down.

When it comes to violence, the numbers are even more revealing. As an *LA [Los Angeles] Times* op/ed pointed out last week [February/March 2007], rape stats have plunged since the '70s. The U.S. Justice Department's National Crime Victimization Survey estimated that 105,000 women were raped in 1973, compared with 30,000 in the latest survey. All indicators of sexual violence are down, and the decrease is most dramatic among younger women. In the past 12 years, according to the survey, sexual victimization rates have fallen 78 percent.

If girls are more hyper-sexualized than ever, and objectification leads inexorably to depression and violence, why are girls achieving at such high rates?

In isolation, those trends don't say anything particularly interesting about the purported connection between short skirts and violence. But rape stats in free fall should at least call into question the casual conflation of Bratz dolls and child abuse. If girls are more hyper-sexualized than ever, and objectification leads inexorably to depression and violence, why are girls achieving at such high rates? It may be that a passel of miniature thongs is contributing to violent behavior. (And at this point, shouldn't we just be impressed that they're sporting underwear at all?) But it's not obvious, and pointing at a bunch of fourth graders in belly shirts does not make it so.

You could as easily tell the opposite story—one in which those thongs are the sartorial equivalent of girl power. Prostitot culture could be the anti-rape, encouraging girls to take control of their sexuality before others do. It's not likely, but the narrative is no more divorced from reality, or bereft of explanatory power, than its APA-stamped counterpart.

Without any mechanism to explain the process by which precocious fashion taste turns to self-loathing, it's probably safest to assume that the kid's department at [JC]Penney and the darkest recesses of American culture exist a world apart. Girls, as they always have, will alternately embrace the trappings of girlhood and struggle against the mythologies of gender. Parents and soi-disant [self-styled] experts will continue to cluck their tongues, and possibly publish papers. Objecting to the fashion choices of the young is perfectly natural. While girls may be baring more skin than ever, the need to dress disapproval as social science says less about their pathologies than it does about ours.

7

Feminists Are to Blame for the Sexualization of Girls

Joseph A. D'Agostino

Joseph A. D'Agostino is vice president for communications at the Population Research Institute. This group is a nonprofit research organization that aims to expose the myth of overpopulation, to expose human rights abuses committed in population control programs, and to make the case that people are the world's greatest resource.

Feminism is to blame for the current crisis of the sexualization of girls. Feminism devalues domesticity and actually promotes the sexual objectification of women by teaching girls that chastity is oppressive. Feminist-thinking men are also the most sexist and predatory, treating women on equal grounds and assuming that women, like them, only desire sex. Men, however, cannot be blamed for having a sexual response to sexualized women. Consumerism creates an additional problem in today's hypersexualized climate. Consumerism turns everything into an object of gratification. Coupled with feminism, which makes promiscuity seem natural, consumer culture treats sex as nothing more than a business transaction. Commitment and marriage are no longer fashionable today, and girls are more interested in improving their bodies than their minds.

Missing from the American Psychological Association's [APA's] report last month [February 2007] about the sexualization of girls, and the media coverage of it, was

Joseph A. D'Agostino, "Feminism, Consumerism, & the Sexualization of Girls," Population Research Organization, March 2, 2007. Copyright © 2007 Population Research Institute (PRI). Reproduced by permission.

feminism's responsibility for this cultural disaster, which is currently harming severely the psyches of tens of millions of American young women. The politically correct view is that the sexualization of girls and feminism are opposing forces, but in fact, they have gone hand in hand. And, according to the report, men today have exchanged "domesticity" for "sexy" in what most find the most attractive quality in a woman. Doesn't that do a lot to explain the decline in the American family and our below-replacement birthrate?

But valuing domesticity in women is so oppressive!

Feminism Objectifies Women

More than 30 years after feminism's triumph, prepubescent girls can be seen regularly in public dressed in miniskirts. Instead of seeking to emulate domestic-oriented women, presenting themselves as future virtuous wives and mothers, little girls seek to emulate Paris Hilton. Children's dolls are made-up to look like prostitutes. "Toy manufacturers produce dolls wearing black leather miniskirts, feather boas, and thigh-high boots and market them to 8- to 12-year-old girls," the APA noted. "Clothing stores sell thongs sized for 7- to 10-year-old girls, some printed with slogans such as 'eye candy' or 'wink wink'; other thongs sized for women and late-adolescent girls are imprinted with characters from Dr. Seuss and the Muppets. In the world of child beauty pageants, five-year-old girls wear fake teeth, hair extensions, and makeup and are encouraged to 'flirt' onstage by batting their long, false eyelashes. On prime-time television, girls can watch fashion shows in which models made to resemble little girls wear sexy lingerie."

Back in college in the early 1990s, I first noticed that it was the feminist men who most objectified women. I was a member of a fraternity, so I had considerable opportunity to observe various types of college men discuss and pursue women. With few exceptions, those men who loudly proclaimed their feminist beliefs and advocated complete equality between the sexes, believing women should be just as career-oriented as men and the like, had the most predatory attitudes. They were interested in sleeping with as many women as possible, as quickly as possible. The more conservative fellows generally slept around less and were more interested in building long-term relationships.

> *Instead of seeking to emulate domestic-oriented women*
> *... little girls seek to emulate Paris Hilton.*

For those who believe in the illusions created by intellectuals and their media sycophants, this is counterintuitive. Aren't conservative, sexist men the ones who are supposed to view women as sex objects? After I puzzled over this quandary for a while, I realized that the natural result of feminism plus consumerism was the sexual objectification of women.

You see, the feminist young men viewed women as being more or less just like them. And what they wanted most from these equals was sex. They had no religious or ethical concerns about chastity, and not many about the sanctity of female sexuality or the fragility of female psychology concerning sex, and regarded their relationships with females as transactional. After all, they didn't force women to sleep with them. It was just a question of getting what they wanted from them, just as one man in business seeks to get what he wants from another in a business transaction.

Men Cannot Be Blamed

My professional life in Washington has taught me the same lesson. The liberal, feminist men in their 20s and 30s that I have known tend to be the most predatory; the conservative, religious ones much less so. Even when it comes to top politicians, the pattern holds. What conservative Republican of the past 20 years can you name who has whored around like [former president] Bill Clinton and [the late Massachusetts senator] Ted Kennedy? I'm not claiming conservative Republican congressmen and senators have been models of virtue—far from it. But they've got a much better record on this question than the other side.

Feminists have taught girls and women that chastity is oppressive, that they should liberate themselves. They have also taught that there are no natural limits to sexuality. Witness their enthusiastic embrace of homosexuality. So, based on feminist principles, why shouldn't little girls sexualize themselves? And why shouldn't adult men and women view them as sexual if there is no such thing as unnatural sexuality?

If you constantly bombard boys with sexualized images of girls and the message "girls are the same as boys" in countless different forms, the primal drive of male sexuality will lead them to prey on girls. Since they're told male and female psychology is the same, the girls must be just as eager to have sex as they are—they just need a little convincing, or a little alcohol or drugs, to loosen up from social constraints. It's really very simple.

Don't get me wrong. I'm not some self-hating male-basher who views every girl who has sexual relations as somehow a victim of male aggression, even if she consents to sex. Up to 40% of rape allegations are completely bogus. There are just as many morally reprehensible women out there as men. There are many girls around these days eager to have sex with boys, and some even seduce the males rather than wait for the reverse. They have a degraded mentality. But so do men and boys who view every attractive female as primarily a sex object.

Of course, when a girl or woman goes around exposing half of her body, how can men and boys be blamed for viewing her as a sex object? A woman's naked legs or midriff triggers a biological sexual response in most men. It's called nature.

Thus is the confluence of two powerful social forces, consumerism and feminism. The first makes us view everything in the world as an object of gratification and every relationship as transactional, and the second makes promiscuity easy and seem natural—feminism puts men and women into the consumerist category when it comes to sex. Of course, the unconditional commitment that marriage used to imply is no longer fashionable. Since sexuality is such a powerful primal force, especially for the young, this consumerist sexuality becomes a huge part of their lives. It's obvious that women tend to suffer more psychologically from this arrangement.

Girls Are Focused on Their Bodies

Indeed, the APA report links sexualization of girls to the three most common psychological problems girls experience: eating disorders, low self-esteem, and depression. Even the rage for unnaturally thin women is reminiscent of desire for the prepubescent body. What is the media leading us to?

Lest you think it has been always thus, just in a different form, the APA report mentions a very interesting study of girls' diaries. First, the report says, "A focus on physical attractiveness is not new; over three decades ago, [a researcher] argued that physical beauty can translate into power for girls. But the definition of attractiveness differs depending on the tastes of the culture. Whereas yesterday's culture may have equated 'domesticity' with attractiveness in women, today's culture equates 'sexy' with attractiveness. . . ."

When a girl or woman goes around exposing half her body, how can men and boys be blamed for viewing her as a sex object?

Of course, feminists have always deplored domesticity. The woman who may be our next president [Hillary Clinton] famously dismissed those women who "stayed at home and baked cookies." Yet, if men used to find "domesticity" attractive, doesn't that imply they were interested in forming lifelong relationships with women that included home, family, and children? Now, men find "sexy" most attractive instead. What does that imply interest in?

The report continues, "Moreover, there is evidence that physical appearance was not always the prime currency for girls' social success. [A researcher in 1997] examined diaries of adolescent girls in the United States over the past 100 years to explore how they discussed self-improvement. Whereas girls of earlier eras focused on improving their studies and becoming more well-mannered, in the last 20 years that [were] studied, girls almost exclusively described changing their bodies and enhancing their physical appearance as the focus of their self-improvement."

That's right. Back in the bad ol' pre-feminist days, when women were so oppressed, teen girls were concerned with getting better grades and improving their social graces. Now, they want to look hot. Write Gloria Steinem [a leader in the feminist movement] today and thank her for what's she done for America's girls.

8

Legislators Need to Do More to Protect Children from Sexual Exploitation

Mary Graw Leary

Mary Graw Leary is an associate professor in the Columbus School of Law at the Catholic University of America in Washington, D.C. Leary is the former deputy director for the Office of Legal Counsel at the National Center for Missing and Exploited Children (NCMEC) and the former director of the National Center for Prosecution of Child Abuse (NCPCA).

The United States must work on multiple fronts to protect children against sexual exploitation. The online sexual exploitation of children is increasing every year, and child pornography is a multibillion-dollar industry. The federal government has joined the fight to protect children by passing the PROTECT (Providing Resources, Officers, and Technology to Eradicate Cyber Threat to) Our Children Act of 2008. The proliferation of pornography and its easy access on the Internet is a special problem that needs to be addressed. The mainstreaming of pornography is also a problem through the glorification of the words pimp *and* pimping *and their accompanying images that today's children view as normal. The national strategy for the PROTECT act must address the role of these social factors, despite certain opposition from free speech advocates and the adult entertainment industry.*

Throughout this last election cycle [in 2008], the media, candidates, and pundits repeatedly reminded us that the nation is in crisis. Indeed, our economy, financial system, and military face severe and complex challenges unseen in over half a century. It is easy, and perhaps wise, in such times to focus on pressing crises. There is a risk, however, that in doing so we will ignore or underestimate other significant challenges. One such challenge is the struggle to protect another' precious resource: our children. In the battle against child sexual exploitation, our nation must fight on multiple fronts for the "hearts and minds" as well as the protection of our children.

The crisis for our youth at this time in our history threatens a generation of Internet-savvy minors. Reported instances of suspected online child sexual exploitation continue every year, surpassing 500,000 such events in 2007. Child pornography is a multibillion-dollar industry, appearing in many media, including on computers and cellular phones, items to which a significant portion of youth have access. Sex trafficking, meanwhile, has been labeled the largest subcategory of modern-day slavery by the State Department. How we as a government and as a society respond to the increased risk of sexual exploitation of children will no doubt have effects long outlasting any one administration.

There is good news. Late last year, the federal government enacted the PROTECT (Providing Resources, Officers, and Technology to Eradicate Cyber Threat to) Our Children Act of 2008. This bipartisan legislation provided numerous measures to combat child sexual exploitation. The bill calls for the establishment of a "National Strategy Child Exploitation Prevention and Interdiction." The act envisions a comprehensive and long-range strategy that seeks to reduce child exploitation through preventative and interdictive approaches. Because of the national strategy's influence on resource allocation and prioritizing programs, the impact of this strategy will be profound. The goals outlined for the strategy are ambitious, but commensurate with the national treasure to be protected: our nation's children.

The legislation allows the attorney general one year to submit the initial strategy to Congress (which will be resubmitted every two years). It requires the strategy to include comprehensive long-range goals for child sexual exploitation reduction as well as measurable objectives designed to meet the aforementioned goals. The Department of Justice must review past policies and work as well as plan future programs relating to child exploitation. These include its interjurisdictional coordination with international, federal, state, local and private sector entities on both prevention and interdiction. The act notably includes directives on prevention, the collection of comprehensive data on the current crisis, and consideration of future trends and challenges. The attorney general is tasked with not only executing this broad vision, but also selecting a senior official responsible for coordinating and developing the national strategy. The act also allots one year for the National Institute of Justice to prepare and submit a report to Congress identifying investigative factors that reliably indicate the level of risk of potential offenders.

How we ... respond to the increased risk of sexual exploitation of children will no doubt have effects long outlasting any one administration.

Social Influences Contribute to Child Sexual Exploitation

The importance of developing this strategy and report makes 2009 a critical year for our children. It is not novel for presidents or cabinet officials to possess authority of broad magnitude, potentially affecting the lives of numerous citizens. Indeed, the secretary of defense has the lives of our service members in his hands and the secretary of health and human services develops policies directly affecting the well-being of millions of vulnerable people. However, the implications of this strategy potentially exceed even these precedents. To develop a flawed strategy is to risk losing a generation. Consequently, by focusing on prevention and cross-jurisdictional coordination, the act allows the attorney general not just to respond to the problem of child sexual exploitation with penological solutions, but also to address the broader atmosphere surrounding such exploitation.

Child sexual exploitation is a complex problem occurring in many forms. While it is criminal to exploit a child sexually, the temptation to focus narrowly on reactive criminal penalties must be resisted. The problem is more than an issue of criminality and penological response. Children are not victimized in a vacuum. Certain societal realities exist that permit the conceptualization of children as sexual objects to be consumed for adult arousal. Any comprehensive review of both the problem and its solution is of little value if it fails to assess the climate in which we live.

Many social influences contribute to child sexual exploitation. I focus on the realities of increasing sexualization of children and objectification of persons manifested through both popular culture media and pornography. These forces can legitimize treating others as commodities—as means to an end—permitting society to be desensitized to the sexual objectification even of young children. These confusing cultural messages can also weaken children's abilities to deflect such exploitation and influence their self-conceptualization as such objects.

While the "adult sex industry" asserts that the expansion of pornography and its increasing social acceptance has only positive effects on society, a growing body of analysis suggests that today's pornography increasingly depicts violent sex acts involving men dominating women. While there is no unanimity in studies of the effects of pornography, recent meta-analysis has found "substantial data showing pornography correlates with various negative outcomes," including increased risk for sexual deviancy, difficulty in intimate relationships, and damage to family life. Additionally, the blurring of the line between legal adult pornography and child pornography is apparent in the explicit marketing of pornography with youthful-looking models in settings with youth-based themes.

To develop a flawed strategy is to risk losing a generation.

A growing body of research comments on the potential negative effects of the proliferation of pornography on juveniles. "Evidence indicates that pornography and related sexual media can influence sexual violence, sexual attitudes, moral values, and sexual activity of children and youth." The existence of the Internet means that children, previously unexposed to such material, are now surrounded by it. Today's youth have access to the Internet and with that access, if unrestricted, comes unlimited access (wanted or not) to countless pornographic Web sites. Because pornography patterns are established during adolescence and rapidly develop in early adulthood, experts argue that accessing pictures and text with degrading or exploitive sexual content may adversely impact the sexual and emotional development of children, or function as a catalyst causing them to act in sexually problematic ways.

The "Pornification" of America

It is not only the substance of contemporary pornography that is problematic, but also the direction of its migration into mainstream society. What is happening to our society has been referred to as "pornification" or "pornographication." As Pamela Paul documents in her examination of pornography in contemporary American culture, *Pornified: How Pornography Is Damaging Our Lives, Our Relationships, and Our Families*, pornography has evolved into the "norm," no longer residing on the fringes of social acceptability. Indeed, a recent study concluded that pornography's acceptance among young adults has reached unprecedented levels. This is true notwithstanding its increase in violence and depictions of male domination over women. Pornography has reached "near mainstream status in American culture." Consider children's pimp and prostitute Halloween costumes; the glorification of the words "pimp" and "pimping" as acceptable in award-winning music titles, prime-time television programming and films; media featuring college-age women's and teens' drunken debauchery; and Internet Web sites counting down the minutes until teen idols obtain the age of eighteen.

The logical inference from these anecdotal realities is supported by growing research and analysis. The American Psychological Association (APA) has documented the deleterious effects of media in its *Report [of the APA Task Force] on the Sexualization of Girls*. The APA cautions that the content of mainstream media is potentially damaging to girls. The potential cognitive effect of this material is a self-objectification in which chronic attention is given to physical appearance, thus leaving fewer cognitive resources for other mental or physical activities. The mental effects can include eating disorders, low self-esteem, and depression. Finally, far from leading to a healthy sexual development, the APA reports that sexual objectification leads to a diminished sexual understanding.

These are just a few of the factors affecting the sexual objectification and exploitation of children. Such effects influence both the demand and supply aspects of exploitation. A challenge for the national strategy is to respond comprehensively. To do this, it must assess the societal climate allowing the sexual objectification of children. The strategy need not debate the value of this material to adults, but must acknowledge the direct and indirect effects on our children and explore constitutional ways to protect them.

To include these realities in a national strategy will require fortitude. First, to comment on the role of mainstream media and increasingly mainstream pornography is to invoke certain wrath from some absolutist free speech advocates. Indeed, the constitutional questions must be examined. However, the Constitution should not be used as a reason to forbid even examining these difficult questions. Rather, it should be used with other tools to inform a thoughtful and considered analysis of these contemporary challenges.

Second, to do so will mean to come into direct conflict with the powerful adult entertainment industry's bottom line. This is a highly profitable industry whose own trade association, the Free Speech Coalition, has a mission to "protect and support the growth and well-being of the adult entertainment community." The "Vision Statement" of the Free Speech Coalition includes unabashedly becoming "a national association that helps limit the legal risks of being an adult business [and] increases the profitability of its members." With such goals, the trade association boasts "the adult Internet is the fastest expanding segment of the U.S. adult entertainment market, having grown from a $1 billion dollar industry in 2002 to a $2.5 billion industry today. . . . The number of adult entertainment Web sites . . . was more than 17 times greater in 2004 than it was just four years earlier, surging from approximately 88,000 in 2000 to nearly 1.6 million sites in 2004." An industry with such a financial stake will be a formidable opponent to any strategy that seeks at least to acknowledge the presence of such material as having deleterious effects on society and on children.

The risks of sexual exploitation appear to be on the rise, making our moment unparalleled in its importance to our culture and children. One year has been allotted to develop an initial strategy that will direct government action and affect our societal and cultural responses to a critical problem documented by researchers, scholars, authors, and professional associations of all disciplines. The person selected to coordinate this effort must be sensitive to the limits of government's ability to solve all social ills, but at the same time bold and courageous enough to outline all the direct and indirect contributors to child sexual exploitation. President [Barack] Obama stated in his weekly radio address the day after assuming office that 2009 commences "in the midst of an unprecedented crisis that calls for unprecedented action." At the end of January he called for "bold" action for the economy. The same must also be true for our children.

9

Mothers Should Resist Norms That Lead to the Sexualization of Girls

Debra Curtis

Debra Curtis is an assistant professor of anthropology at Salve Regina University in Newport, Rhode Island. She writes frequently on adolescence and sexuality, has served as a media programming consultant for NBC, and has been interviewed about female sexuality by the Pittsburgh Tribune-Review *and the* New York Times.

Pedophiles are parents' worst nightmares, and they are ordinary men, usually men in children's everyday lives. Pedophiles eroticize children, viewing them as objects for their sexual pleasure. While mothers fear pedophiles, many mothers are contributing to the eroticizing of their own children by allowing them to dress provocatively. To many young girls, being fashionable means dressing sexy, and parents are allowing it, essentially trading their girls' innocence for sexuality. Mothers need to both resist and change the cultural norms that teach girls that looking good means looking sexy.

It is probably a good idea, right off the bat, to tell you a bit about myself. I am a cultural anthropologist, a mother of 9-year-old twin girls, and the wife of a doctor. My research focuses on how popular culture influences sexuality.

When I was younger I was not seduced by pop culture. Some may find that hard to believe. Trust me when I tell you,

Debra Curtis, "The Sexualization of Girls," *Providence Journal*, January 2, 2008. Copyright © 2008 The Providence Journal. Reproduced by permission.

as an anthropologist who fully understands the constraining aspects of culture, that I lived on the edges of normative society, sometimes intentionally. My refusal to shave my legs for more than a decade might have cost me the title of "Homecoming Queen." I'm not kidding. I was first runner-up. I know what you are thinking, "I wonder what the other girls looked like."

Besides trying to defy the dominant rules of femininity, I also never got wrapped up in television shows and rarely went to rock concerts. I was, as you might have guessed, culturally retarded. Now I follow trends in popular culture as a meteorologist tracks weather patterns. I like to think of myself as an anthropologist-psychic, foretelling how popular culture will influence our sexual practices and desires.

Recently, I was listening to an interview on NPR [National Public Radio]. The guest was a photographer whose latest exhibit features morbidly obese nude women. Leonard Nimoy, known to the world as Mr. Spock, turned out to be the guest photographer. And viewers of *Star Trek* know that Mr. Spock is known for making prophetic and insightful comments. I was enthralled, listening attentively, when the NPR host asked Nimoy to talk about what inspired him as an artist. Nimoy replied that he was once told to "move toward what scares you."

A few days later, while I was having lunch with two colleagues—a philosopher and a social psychologist—I was reminded of what it is that scares me most: pedophiles.

Like many parents, the fear of someone forcing my young daughters to have sex runs deep and has the potential to turn me into a madwoman.

Inevitably, our lunch conversations turn to the subject matters we are lecturing about that day. On that afternoon, I had prepared a lecture based on my fieldwork on Nevis, a small island in the Caribbean, in which I addressed the topic of sexual-economic exchange, in particular the way young girls trade sexual favors with older men for access to goods and cash. The philosopher explained that his students were in the middle of reading *Lolita*, by Vladimir Nabokov [a story about a pedophile], which has been hailed as one of the best 100 books ever written. I confessed, between bites of my sandwich, that I had never read it. This came as a shock to my colleague, who understood all too well the nature of my research on girls and sex in the Caribbean. He tried to persuade me to read *Lolita*, exclaiming, "Wouldn't you, of all people, want to understand the mind of a man who wants to have sex with a young girl, if not for your research, then to protect your daughters?" I could hear Mr. Spock's voice, "move toward what scares you."

Like many parents, the fear of someone forcing my young daughters to have sex runs deep and has the potential to turn me into a madwoman. I must admit, while up until that moment in my life, I had not yet worked up the nerve to read *Lolita*, I used to watch NBC's *To Catch a Predator*, an evening program that sets up sting operations to catch sexual predators. It fascinated me. I studied the faces of the men on my high-definition TV, reminding myself and anyone else who would listen, namely my students and girlfriends, that pedophiles are ordinary-looking men, sometimes strangers, but more often than not, men who are in our everyday lives.

Mothers Are Trading Their Daughters' Innocence for Sexuality

Men who prefer prepubescent girls sexualize them. In the eyes of a pedophile, girls are highly eroticized objects for their sexual pleasure. Part of what makes young girls so attractive to pedophiles is their innocence, or what some call their sexual naivete. I can say without a doubt that 99 percent of mothers would just as soon cut off their right arms as permit their daughters to be alone in a room with a known pedophile.

And yet, these same mothers are seduced by, and let their daughters be seduced by, the demands of our popular culture, which sexualizes girls. We all know what this looks like—preteens dressed as young adults, the 6- to 10-year-old set wearing cropped tight-fitted T-shirts, low-cut jeans, jewelry and lip gloss—oversized and hyper-sexed Bratz dolls. The message is clear, "looking fashionable means looking sexy." On the positive side, a slow but growing social commentary is critical of this unhealthy trend. My personal favorite is *Stop Dressing Your Six-Year-Old Like a Skank*.

Mothers are trading their daughters' innocence for a type of sexuality that is potentially very dangerous.

Experts tell us that children who have been molested often live with depression, eating disorders and low self-esteem, all of which, negatively impact the quality of their lives. Guess what? A team of psychologists recently reported that exposing prepubescent girls to a media culture that teaches them to be prematurely sexual is also strongly associated with depression, eating disorders and low self-esteem.

Critical of the sexualization of girls, Rosa Brooks, in the *Los Angeles Times*, wrote that capitalism is "busy serving our children up to pedophiles on corporate platters." I would add that many mothers are acting as the caterers. I'm not talking about the JonBenét Ramsey beauty-pageant mothers; that's a given. I am pointing my finger at the mothers who buy their 6- to 10-year-olds platform shoes, short leopard-print skirts, and the children's version of the bikini swimsuits seen in Victoria's Secret catalogs. I am pointing my finger at the mother who doesn't say no when her preteen begs her to let her get her ears pierced—and who then allows her to wear dangly earrings.

The Power of Culture

Every semester, I drag out sensational stories from my anthropological toolbox to teach my students about the power of culture. We read about mothers who bound their daughters' feet in 19th-century China, a brutal act representing submission to larger cultural influences. We learn about impoverished Thai parents who trade their daughters for television sets, and their little girls end up as child prostitutes.

While doing fieldwork in the Caribbean on girls' sexuality, I collected stories about Nevisian mothers who sell their young daughters to men for sex. But here too, in the United States, mothers are trading their daughters' innocence for a type of sexuality that is potentially very dangerous. Are American mothers any less complicit in their daughters' subordination when they dress them like [celebrities] Britney [Spears] or Paris [Hilton]? When we buy into the rules set by popular culture, when we believe that our daughters have to dress like celebrities, when we limit their choices in life by teaching them early on that looking good always means looking sexy, we are seeing them through the eyes of pedophiles.

I am not arguing that when mothers dress their preteens provocatively they are asking for trouble from pedophiles. That's not it. I believe that this world should be safe enough for women to dress as they please. The key word here is "women." I understand why many mothers dress their daughters in the latest inappropriate fashions. It reflects the same complicated reasons why I enroll my daughters in private golf and piano lessons, drive a gas-guzzling SUV [sport-utility vehicle] and take pride in my husband's occupation—it speaks to the desire to fit in and present the proper social markers of status and prestige. But take it from a woman who did not shave her legs for most of the '80s—we can resist dominant cultural norms. More importantly, we must change them.

10

Fathers Should Not Exploit Their Daughters' Sexuality

Rebecca Traister

Rebecca Traister is a senior writer at Salon. *She writes extensively about women in entertainment and politics, and she has also covered the New York film business. Her writing has appeared in* Elle, *the* New York Times, GQ, Allure, *and* Mademoiselle.

Fifteen-year-old television and pop star Miley Cyrus found herself at the center of controversy in 2008 when she appeared, scantily clad, on the cover of Vanity Fair. *The public outrage in response to this photo seems exaggerated when one considers how Cyrus has already been packaged and marketed as a cultural commodity. American society sends a double message to young girls. The media tells them they need to look and act sexy, yet they are censored when they become mature enough to really understand and express their sexuality. Billy Ray Cyrus's role in his daughter's photo shoot is what is really disturbing. He profits from Miley's continuing exposure in the press, and the provocative pictures of father and daughter give a boost to his masculine image. It is wrong for Cyrus and other celebrity fathers to treat their daughters' sexuality as their personal property.*

I've been home sick for part of this week, and I'll admit to logging some couch time with my favorite daily tabloid of choice, the dastardly *New York Post*.

And that's how, even in my lozenge-soothed stupor, I learned of this week's [April 2008] major celebrity scandal: the purportedly jaw-dropping Annie Leibovitz photos of partially unclothed 15-year-old *Hannah Montana* star Miley Cyrus in the upcoming issue of *Vanity Fair*.

I looked at the pictures of her in the weird back-baring stole thing. I agreed with my colleague Sarah Hepola that you generally see more skin at prom, and that this smacks of the kind of "Outrage!" often voiced by those who cheerfully participate in questionable pop culture habits—like consuming teen sexuality as served up by every television network, magazine, record company and movie studio—until the moment at which a large national spotlight is shone on them. Then they scream "Eek!" and start preaching about values.

We send the message to young girls that their job and their worth as young women will depend on their ability to look and act sexy.

Sure, Cyrus is being sexualized, and I guess it's all kind of gross. But come on—in a world in which we market push-up bras ... to preadolescents and tweens, in which *Vanity Fair* throws naked or lingerie-encased women on its covers whenever possible—are we really *so* appalled by the sight of a less-clad-than-usual 15-year-old who has already been packaged, marketed and unrelentingly sold, sold and sold to America's daughters?

This is but one of the problems with how we treat developing female sexuality in this country: With every Barbie, every Abercrombie & Fitch catalog, every music video and every new style of miniskirt and tube top made in junior sizes and worn on *Hannah Montana*, we send the message to young girls that their job and their worth as young women will depend on their ability to look and act sexy, preferably while mouthing words they don't yet understand about virginity and purity. Then, when they get to an age at which they might exhibit feelings or behaviors related to actual sex, we castigate and censor them.

It's undoubtedly a deeply troubling and twisted cycle of hypocrisy and mixed messages, one that is worth examining, but not via faux [false] puritanical outrage over a stole-wrapped teenager, especially when that teenager is owned and operated by a corporation currently selling racy underwear to children in China.

Fathers Do Not Own Their Daughters' Bodies

But what is mystifying to me about the whole mess: Why the outcry over the nude-back photo and very little uproar over the truly upsetting shot of Cyrus with her daddy, Billy Ray? To me this image, in which daughter slumps on father's lap, his hand holding hers, her nearly exposed hip jutting out just next to his arm, is far more suggestive than the tousled back-less image, which at least leaves open the possibility that this young woman might be trying out her sexual agency on her own, not playing it up to enhance *her father's* masculinity. Yech. The image, in fact, is shiveringly reminiscent of less artsy-fartsy recent photos of Miley acting foolish with her *boyfriend*.

But the still image of Miley and Billy Ray has nothing on the very much more creepy behind-the-scenes video of the photo shoot, currently available on *Vanity Fair*'s Web site. In it, the Cyruses—père et fille [father and daughter]—are shown posing together, his hand resting on her inner thigh as he nuzzles her forehead and she gazes up at him adoringly. The camera skims up her legs as her dad simultaneously throws his arm around her protectively and does his best Le Tigre for Leibovitz's camera, which is, after all, resuscitating his career at the same time it frames and captures his offspring's blossoming allure. Talk about boosting your own credentials on the body (literally) of your daughter.

And it's not just this Cyrus thing.

How about these stomach-turning images of Hulk Hogan caressing his bikini-clad daughter Brooke?

And in this week's other *New York Post* scandal, about baseball star Roger Clemens' reported affair with country singer Mindy McCready, whom he met when she was 15 (she is now 32), I couldn't help noticing that McCready's father acted as her spokesman, and was comfortable clarifying—not to say publicizing—details of his daughter's sexual past to a newspaper. "I've been talking to Mindy about this a lot, and I can assure you that nothing went on between them physically until well after she had moved to Nashville," Tim McCready assured the *Post*, adding that "with Roger, there was a definite attraction between them. But it was an on-again, off-again thing. . . . For Roger, once spring training comes around and the season starts, he is dedicated to baseball. So they had about three months a year when they could see each other."

Bleaaargh.

How about, instead of slapping the wrists of those (*Vanity Fair*, Disney, the Cyrus family) who will blush or wag their fingers all the way to the bank thanks to this Cyrus story, we take a moment to make a salient point: Family values—as defined by Walt Disney, the Church, the Republican Party or anyone else—do not include a father's ownership of his daughter's body or sexuality, or his treatment of her sexuality as his property or financial or personal resource.

11

The Sexualization of Teen Celebrities Is Ethically Questionable

Jack Marshall

Jack Marshall is the founder and president of ProEthics, an ethics training and consulting firm in Alexandria, Virginia. Marshall is the primary writer and editor for Ethics Scoreboard, an ethics and opinion Web site. He writes on leadership, ethics, popular culture, and other topics, and his commentary has been featured on numerous radio and television programs.

Many people are to blame for the controversy surrounding Miley Cyrus's provocative 2008 cover photo for Vanity Fair. First, the magazine itself failed to show sound ethical judgment by exploiting the teen star's sexuality. Famed photographer Annie Leibovitz likewise suffered a lapse in judgment by not considering Cyrus's youth and vulnerability when she orchestrated the photo shoot. Cyrus's family and her professional representatives failed her by not protecting her from being sexually exploited and by burdening her with a public apology for the photographs after the controversy erupted. Celebrities in the American media do not help matters by brushing off the Cyrus incident as no big deal. However, the early sexualization of Miley Cyrus and other teen stars ripples through American culture. Young girls who idolize these stars want to be just like them, even if that means acting or dressing in ways that are sexually exploitive.

It should cause ethical whiplash. Here is former teen comet Britney Spears, still not sufficiently stable to have control of her own financial affairs or to see her children regularly, trying to rebuild her shattered reputation with a guest role on a TV sitcom. Here she is posing with her apparently proudly pregnant little sister [Jamie Lynn Spears], whose own bubbly tween show is once again running on cable's Nickelodeon. Here is Dina Lohan being honored as a "Mother of the Year," as she relentlessly pushes her 14-year-old daughter [Ali] down the same path that led older daughter Lindsay to nude magazine photo shoots and rehab stays just a few years after her last Disney movie. And here is 15-year-old Miley Cyrus, Disney's squeaky clean and wholesome Hannah Montana, posing for *Vanity Fair* in poses that make her look like an aspiring Lolita . . . especially one that appears to show her naked, wrapped only in a bedsheet.

The revelation of the photos, taken by famed (and reliably provocative) photographer Annie Leibovitz, ignited a multifront controversy. Disney, seeing its wholesome meal ticket being prematurely sexualized, regarded the photos as an affront to its audience and bottom line. Miley Cyrus apologized, suggesting she was pressured and duped by the magazine and Leibovitz to take photos she was now ashamed of. *Vanity Fair* pointed out that Cyrus's parents and advisors were on hand throughout the shoot. Leibovitz commented, sadly, that she was sorry her innocent photo was being misunderstood, as it was just "a simple, classic portrait."

Of course, Leibovitz probably thought her *Vanity Fair* cover photo of Demi Moore naked and pregnant was a simple classic portrait. But to some people who would not normally be called hysterics, photographs of seminude 15-year-old girls looking as if they [have] just been deflowered are called "child porn."

Bad Judgment, Irresponsibility, and Hypocrisy

There is almost too much dishonesty, bad judgment, irresponsibility and hypocrisy to catalogue in the Cyrus-*Vanity Fair* "scandal." Some of it, however, is easy to grade in ethics terms:

Vanity Fair: Exploiting the sexuality of a 15-year-old girl to sell magazines is obviously not regarded as an illegitimate strategy in the editorial offices, and its effect on the psyche of the teenager involved, her career, her reputation, or the attitudes of her young fans is simply not on the magazine's radar screen. In other words, there is no ethical consideration here at all. **Ethics Grade: F**

Photographer Annie Leibovitz: Ditto. In her case, all that matters is continuing her reign as America's edgiest, most talked about celebrity photographer. Cyrus? To Leibovitz, she's like a bowl of fruit to a painter, a lump of clay to a sculptor, or an electric guitar to a rock singer: just a means to an end. The only difference is that you don't have to persuade bowls of fruit, lumps of clay or guitars to be an artist's means to an end. The fact that Miley Cyrus is a human being and a very young and vulnerable one evidently doesn't enter into the equation for Leibovitz. Again, there was no ethical reasoning going on behind the camera, none at all. **Ethics Grade: F**

To some people who would not normally be called hysterics, photographs of seminude 15-year-old girls looking as if they [have] just been deflowered are called "child porn."

Billy Ray Cyrus and others: Not that it excuses *Vanity Fair*'s conduct, but Miley Cyrus was failed by those the law and nature hold as her guardians and protectors: her parents and professional representatives. Not only did Papa Cyrus not prevent exploitive and disturbing photos of his daughter, he participated in one that depicts his relationship with his daughter in a sexually suggestive manner. The father of the teen superstar, perhaps to enhance his own career visibility, was a full participant in the sexualization of his daughter's image. Then he allowed his daughter to do the public apologizing. **Ethics Grade: F minus**

The Excusers: Many show business types, from Regis Philbin and Kelly Ripa to Rosie O'Donnell, weighed in with the opinion that the whole flap was over nothing, that the photo was nothing to get upset about. The general thrust of their arguments was a version of one of the [Ethics] Scoreboard's least favorite rationalizations: "This isn't the worst thing." Yes, it's true: a photo of Cyrus naked and frolicking with a goat would be worse, for example. It isn't Lindsay Lohan's mug shot, and Cyrus isn't an unwed mother like Jamie Lynn Spears. The fact that we can imagine worse doesn't make it healthy for Cyrus and the culture for her to be portrayed, while still a child, in a sexually suggestive pose. As for those who deny that it is a sexually suggestive pose, they are either being dishonest, dense, or working in Hollywood simply obliterates any sense of shock or outrage. These are the people who refuse to draw any ethical lines at all, encouraging values and public sensitivity to inappropriate conduct to dissolve into vapors. **Ethics Grade: F**

The Sexualization of Teen Celebrities Impacts Teen Culture

You will find no criticism here of Miley Cyrus, who is a minor trying to cope with the dazzling, corrupting and confusing world of big-money entertainment at an age when most kids are making extra money babysitting. Who knows what advice she is getting, and from whom? The journey from innocent child star to adult actress is extremely perilous and uncertain, and competition is fierce. Who in Hollywood that can be counted upon to argue will say that *7th Heaven* star Jessica Biel's decision to pose topless for a skanky men's magazine while still regarded as a "good girl" teen role model wasn't a better career tactic than the decision of Larisa Oleynik, then the star of a Nickelodeon hit, to make her film debut playing another squeaky clean teen? Today Oleynik is a working actress but hardly a star, while Biel is a full-fledged *femme fatale* superstar. It is a good bet that Cyrus has been hearing that she needs to start attracting male stalkers before it's too late.

The early sexualization of TV actresses whose fans are young teens and pre-teens has a strong rippling effect across the culture, encouraging girls to go where their idols appear to be going. In the case of Hannah Montana, their idol is inviting someone to have sex; in the case of Zoey, [the character played by] Jamie Lynn Spears, their idol is actually having a baby. For decades, well before the popular culture became the behavioral juggernaut it is today, it was accepted wisdom that the images and reputations of young girls who were media stars required special protection, so that culturally dangerous messages weren't broadcast to their impressionable fans. Today that wisdom is largely ignored in pursuit of commerce, but it is no less valid.

Miley Cyrus's *Vanity Fair* photograph session once again suggests a question that nobody wants to ask, much less answer: *If young actors make so much money for so many people that their images are inevitably exploited by those who should be looking out for their welfare, and if their visibility and influence as objects of affection and admiration are used to corrupt the values and conduct of our children, why should our culture permit children to work in the entertainment field at all?*

If the entertainment world, the media, and parents do not get serious about preventing both of these by-products of child stardom, and quickly, that question will be asked with increasing intensity and frequency.

12

Corporate Media Sexualizes Young Girls

M. Gigi Durham, as told to Tana Ganeva

Tana Ganeva is an associate editor at AlterNet, an online news magazine. Ganeva's articles frequently cover issues regarding sex, love, and relationships. In the following viewpoint, Ganeva interviews M. Gigi Durham, the author of The Lolita Effect: The Media Sexualization of Young Girls and What We Can Do About It.

The Lolita Effect is the way corporate culture sexualizes young girls by marketing sexualized clothing and behaviors. Little girls, however, should not be marketed to as legitimate sexual actors. Marketing messages make girls think they have to conform to a certain body type and wear certain clothes to look sexy. These messages, which focus on how girls look, negate other important aspects of their personalities. While American culture encourages girls to look sexually desirable, it condemns girls who act out their sexual desires. Boys, on the other hand, are encouraged to see girls as sexual objects. In this light, neither boys, nor girls gain a mutual understanding of sex and sexuality. Society, however, should also understand that children gain the bulk of their understanding about sexuality from the media. Parents should be involved in monitoring their children's media consumption while teaching kids how to be critical consumers.

In 2006, the retail chain Tesco launched the Peekaboo Pole Dancing Kit, a play set designed to help young girls "unleash the sex kitten inside." Perturbed parents, voicing concern that their five-year-olds might be too young to engage in sex work, lobbied to have the product pulled. Tesco removed the play set from the toy section but kept it on the market. As M. Gigi Durham points out in *The Lolita Effect: The Media Sexualization of Young Girls and What We Can Do About It*, Tesco's attempt to sell stripper gear to kids is just one instance of the sexual objectification of young girls in the media and marketplace. Some of the many other examples include a push-up bra for preteens, thongs for 10-year-olds bearing slogans like "eye candy," and underwear geared toward teens with "Who needs credit cards . . . ?" written across the crotch. Targeted by marketers at increasingly younger ages, girls are now being exposed to the kind of unhealthy messages about sexuality that have long dogged grown women. Girls are told that their worth hinges on being "hot," which in mainstream media parlance translates into thin, white, make upped and scantily clad. Meanwhile, acting on their sexual impulses earns them the epithet "slut." Teen magazines advise girls on how to tailor their look and personality to please boys (in order to entrap them in relationships). Advertisements present violence toward women as sexy. According to Durham, the regressive messages about sexuality that circulate in mainstream media hamper the healthy sexual development of kids and teens. Durham's critique does not end with the corporate media. She also faults adults for failing to engage in reasonable, open dialogue with teens about sex—thus leaving the sexual education of young people to a media primarily concerned with generating profit, as opposed to, say, selflessly helping young people develop healthy ideas about sexuality. AlterNet talked to Durham on the phone about the sexual objectification of girls in the media and how to help them challenge regressive messages about their sexuality.

The Lolita Effect

[Alternet]: *What's the "Lolita Effect," and why is it harmful?*

[Durham]: The Lolita Effect is the media's sexual objectification of young girls. In the [Vladimir] Nabokov novel the protagonist, who is 12 years old at the start of the book, is the object of desire for Humbert Humbert the pedophile. In the book you're put into the mind of the predator; Lolita, in Humbert's view, initiates the sex and is very knowledgeable and all that. Nowadays the term Lolita has come to mean a little girl who is inappropriately sexual, wanton, and who sort of flaunts her sexuality and seduces older men. I'm very critical of that construction in the novel and in real life because little girls can't be held responsible in this way. They're not born with the understanding or intention of seducing older men, and the burden of responsibility can't be placed on children. They're just too young to knowingly enter into these kinds of relationships. The Lolita Effect is the way our culture, and more importantly our corporate media, have constructed these little "Lolitas" by sexualizing them and marketing really sexualized items of clothing and behaviors to them—constructing them as legitimate sexual actors when they aren't. . . .

One of the marketing messages geared toward young girls is the idea that being "hot" and "eye candy" for boys is of paramount importance. How does this emphasis on "hotness" hinder girls' development of healthy ideas about sexuality?

Let me say first that I think sex is great. I think sex is a wonderful, totally natural part of growing up. I think children are sexual—and that's not just me; all of the research points to that. Adolescents are trying to understand their sexuality. And I do think that wanting to be sexually desirable is part of being a human being. But at the same time this construction of "hotness" is rigidly and narrowly defined by the media. And there's so much emphasis placed on it that it becomes the only thing that's important in girls' lives—or at least that's what the media would have you believe. Because achieving the mainstream media's version of "hotness" demands being a consumer. If you're trying to be "hot" in the ways that they prescribe—conforming to a specific body type, wearing a certain type of clothing—of course you are going to be spending a lot of money trying to achieve it. So there are problems with it. For one thing, it negates and devalues all of the other aspects of a girl's personality. Sex is good, but it's one aspect of being a human being. A lot of other things are equally important, like your intelligence, creativity, spirituality and community involvement. All of these things are equally important in terms of being a full-fledged human being. But in many media, girls are told that only being hot matters. So it can warp them into skewed, one-dimensional people, where all these other aspects of their personalities aren't being developed. So that hampers them, as people. In terms of sexuality, they can't experience their sexuality fully and joyfully and individually and diversely because they're being held up to this very narrow, very restrictive definition of what sexiness is about. So I think it's problematic on both of those fronts.

The term Lolita has come to mean a little girl who is inappropriately sexual, wanton, and who sort of flaunts her sexuality and seduces older men.

Can you talk about the idea that girls have to be "hot" but not "sluts"? Why do you think that this is such a deeply ingrained, pervasive construct?

That's not new. Girls have had to walk that line for quite a while now, where the emphasis is on being sexually desirable but immediately being condemned if they actually act on their desire. Girls are expected not to have desires of their own. The scholar Deborah L. Tolman identified this—she called it "the missing discourse of girls' desire"—I think sometime in the mid-'80s. This has been a problem for girls and women all along: They have not been allowed to express their own interest in sex or express their own desires or seek their own pleasure for quite a long time. . . . It's a terrible mixed message, and it's almost impossible to achieve it—to walk around projecting desirability but to never be able to act on it, never be allowed to engage in it. One of the other problems is that because of this idea, girls aren't given good information about actual sexual activity. They are not given information to make them understand the risks and responsibilities, how to be in control, protect themselves against STDs [sexually transmitted diseases], unintended pregnancies—that's missing from the way they understand sex.

Is there a comparable set of messages about sexuality aimed at boys?

It's not as pervasive. Here's what I think about boys. I think they're getting a lot of messages about girls as sexual objects, in music videos and in video games. In most of the media targeted to teens and even to tweens, girls are always presented as eye candy and sexual objects. Both boys and girls are getting that message. Now, the message that boys are getting about sexuality and masculinity is that male sexuality is predatory, often violent and not emotionally engaged. Those are problematic constructions too. But in the end, girls bear the brunt of those constructions because they give boys an awful lot of power. They don't really put boys in vulnerable positions; they put boys in more powerful positions. In the end, it harms both boys and girls. They are not getting good information. They're not getting an ethical, mutual understanding of sex and sexuality, where it's about consensus and cooperation and understanding each other on some human level. It's all about predation and submission.

Girls Are Sexual Beings

You emphasize throughout the book that girls are not zombified, unthinking consumers of media but tend to be very critical of media representations. So to a certain extent, these offensive im-

ages and messages must resonate with the desires of many girls. How do we deal with the fact that sometimes sexuality isn't very P.C. [politically correct]?

In the sense of wanting to adopt some of these (sexual) costumes and things like that? I think there is a playful side to it. And I'm not criticizing out of hand. I'm not saying that girls shouldn't wear makeup or high heels. I don't think any of that is true. Because I do think that there is a lot of fun and playfulness involved in some of that. But I do think that girls need to think about it and to make sure that what they're doing is intentional and is making them feel good about themselves and good about their bodies and knowing that they have a lot of different choices. If they want to adopt a certain type of costuming one day that's OK, but they can go out in their baseball hats and blue jeans another day. They should be allowed to make informed choices about how to present themselves to the world, and they need to understand the consequences of those presentations. I think we need to have a lot of discussion about that with girls, just as long as it doesn't become a type of obsession that limits their views of what it means to be a girl. The other side of it for me is that they should always feel like they're safe when they do that. As long as they feel like they're making choices that don't put them in a bad position, and also the adults around them don't feel like they're putting themselves in a vulnerable position. But one of the problems is that for many, many girls those choices are not completely safe, especially if they are in a situation where they could be at physical risk. We just need to be thinking really hard about how they're choosing to make these kinds of moves.

In the book you describe yourself as a pro-sex feminist. How did this perspective inform your approach to the topic?

It was very important to me not to be moralizing and coming across like I was policing or repressing girls' sexuality. I wanted to make it clear from the start that sex is a good thing and a really normal part of being a human being, and that we ought to acknowledge that children and teenagers are sexual and we shouldn't draw back in horror. One of the problems for me is that in the U.S. we have such a puritanical view of sex—we absolutely refuse to talk about it, we don't have good sex-ed in schools, we don't give kids straightforward, accurate information about sex. I wanted to, in a way, redefine the term pro-sex. I'm pro healthy, progressive ideas about sex. And I'm totally opposed to regressive or restrictive ideas about sex. I think that's a little different from the way it's normally defined. . . .

In most of the media targeted to teens and even to tweens, girls are always presented as eye candy and sexual objects.

Sex and Profit

What do you think about the controversy over the new Grand Theft Auto *game?*

I do have issues with violent video games, because the way gender is presented reinscribes these really traditional and polarized views of masculinity and femininity, where men are violent aggressors and the women are almost always presented as sex workers—they're always strippers or prostitutes. So there are almost no women with agency or power, who can command actual respect from men. And again, there aren't men who could work things (nonviolently), for example. So I definitely don't see them as progressive representations.

Can you talk a little more about the profit motive in media that in part drives these regressive representations of sexuality and sexiness?

That's a really key point in my argument. The media are for-profit enterprises, and we need to recognize that from the start. Whatever they do to represent any aspect of human experience, it's going to be connected to generating revenue. When they represent sex and sexuality, very obviously it's going to have a commercial motivation behind it. So we get these definitions of sexuality that are yoked to consumerism, and sexuality is only represented in a way that will stimulate consumption. So they're not acting in girls' best interests, and they're not acting in society's best interests; they're acting to generate profits. We ought to understand that however media represent sexuality is not going to be in ways that are good for anybody but the corporations! What happens, though, is that media are influential in teaching kids about sex. There are studies indicating that because we don't have discussions about sex anywhere else in society—most kids don't get it at school, most of them don't get it at home—kids get a lot of their sexual understanding from the media. So they're going to only get corporate representations. They're not going to get alternative ideas about sexuality or countermessages or scripts that could challenge some of those types of representations.

You also make the point that we can't blame everything on the media. What do you think of the tactics of conservative watchdog groups like the Parents Television Council?

Some of them are very censorious in their approach. I think there are some watchdog groups that are really helpful. One group I go to a lot is Common Sense Media, because I think their movie reviews are good and fair and they give you a lot of information so that you can make decisions about the media. But others are really inclined to repress representations in ways that I think are problematic. So I think we ought to be careful about that. I'm totally opposed to censorship. But I do think that parents could, and should, monitor their kids' media consumption, because not everything is appropriate for children of all ages. Even recently in my own life I've seen little kids traumatized by watching violent media. But you can't keep kids in a bubble forever. As they get older, they're going to be exposed to these things, and the most helpful thing that anyone can do is talk about what's going on in the media with children and offering them ways to maintain distance and be critical of these representations and understanding the selling intentions behind them and all of those things. But I know that not all parents or counselors or teachers are informed enough about media studies or media literacy to be able to bring these things up or to offer these perspectives. So one of the things I argue for in the book is media literacy education in the schools. I really think that in this world it's as important as reading and writing, maybe even more important, for kids to understand the media.

But there's probably about as much funding for that as there is for sex-ed.

Yeah, totally. At the same time I think parents can go to these watchdog organizations, but to use their own judgment in terms of which ones they're going to rely on. They can cobble together different perspectives and make good decisions. And the third thing is, in my book there's a sort of DIY [do-it-yourself] media literacy for everyday people because I think a lot of these analytical strategies in the province of media scholars that are talked about in academic journals and conferences—these never get out to the general public, who need them more than we do. One goal of the book is to offer those strategies to people in the real world.

We ought to understand that however media represent sexuality is not going to be in ways that are good for anybody but the corporations!

Is that basically what you would tell a parent who is concerned about overly sexualized media images, but doesn't want to send the message to their kid that sexuality is bad?

Yes. Share values, talk about them, critique them. What I'm arguing for is the exact opposite of censorship, which is just a lot more critique and public discussion and debate about all of this.

Should we be trying to change the media, or is it best to stick to informing people and kids about it so they become more critical consumers?

To me the most important thing is to develop critical consumers, to put agency in the hands of consumers. There are a lot of interesting groups out there working with the media. For example, there's a group called the Media Project, and they work with TV writers to try to put more factual, more diverse information about sexuality into TV shows; not in a preachy kind of way, but in a way that would expand ideas about sex. The thing I want to emphasize is that any adult can start a conversation with their kids, even when they are really, really young, even as young as 2, which is what I've done with my kids. Not even specifically about sex, but about the selling intent behind advertising and comparing what goes on in real life to fiction and helping them sort out facts. You can start getting them to be critical of the media when they're very young.

13

Gay and Lesbian Children Are Coming Out Earlier

Benoit Denizet-Lewis

Benoit Denizet-Lewis is a contributing writer for New York Times Magazine. *He is the author of* America Anonymous: Eight Addicts in Search of a Life, *and* American Voyeur: Dispatches from the Far Reaches of Modern Life.

Today's young homosexuals are coming out to their communities at an earlier age. Many middle schoolers who are gay can now attend dances and community groups where they find people who are supportive about their sexuality. American middle schools for the most part, however, are not prepared to handle openly gay students. Further, today's gay students face greater obstacles than their straight adolescent peers. Gay middle schoolers have been harassed on campuses nationwide, and many have been assaulted. As a response to this treatment, some schools have formed gay-straight alliances in an effort to open up communication on campus and to keep gay teens safe. Although the formation of these groups has met with opposition on some campuses, gay teens tend to agree that they need a safe, supportive place to be themselves.

Austin didn't know what to wear to his first gay dance last spring. It was bad enough that the gangly 13-year-old from Sand Springs, Okla., had to go without his boyfriend at the time, a 14-year-old star athlete at another middle school, but there were also laundry issues. "I don't have any clean clothes!" he complained to me by text message, his favored method of communication.

When I met up with him an hour later, he had weathered his wardrobe crisis (he was in jeans and a beige T-shirt with musical instruments on it), but was still a nervous wreck. "I'm kind of scared," he confessed. "Who am I going to talk to? I wish my boyfriend could come." But his boyfriend couldn't find anyone to give him a ride nor, Austin explained, could his boyfriend ask his father for one. "His dad would give him up for adoption if he knew he was gay," Austin told me. "I'm serious. He has the strictest, scariest dad ever. He has to date girls and act all tough so that people won't suspect."

Austin doesn't have to play "the pretend game," as he calls it, anymore. At his middle school, he has come out to his close friends, who have been supportive. A few of his female friends responded that they were bisexual. "Half the girls I know are bisexual," he said. He hadn't planned on coming out to his mom yet, but she found out a week before the dance. "I told my cousin, my cousin told this other girl, she told her mother, her mother told my mom and then my mom told me," Austin explained. "The only person who really has a problem with it is my older sister, who keeps saying: 'It's just a phase! It's just a phase!'"

Austin's mom was on vacation in another state during my visit to Oklahoma, so a family friend drove him to the weekly youth dance at the Openarms Youth Project in Tulsa, which is housed in a white cement-block building next to a redbrick Baptist church on the east side of town. We arrived unfashionably on time, and Austin tried to park himself on a couch in a corner, but was whisked away by Ben, a 16-year-old Openarms regular, who gave him an impromptu tour and introduced him to his mom, who works the concession area most weeks.

Openly Gay Teens Can Find Support

Openarms is practically overrun with supportive moms. While Austin and Ben were on the patio, a 14-year-old named Nick arrived with his mom. Nick came out to her when he was 12, but had yet to go on a date or even kiss a boy, which prompted his younger sister to opine that maybe he wasn't actually gay. "She said, 'Maybe you're bisexual,'" Nick told me. "But I don't have to have sex with a girl to know I'm not interested."

I don't think I would have come out if I wasn't popular.

Ninety minutes after we arrived, Openarms was packed with about 130 teenagers who had come from all corners of the state. Some danced to the Lady Gaga song "Poker Face," others battled one another in pool or foosball and a handful of young couples held hands on the outdoor patio. In one corner, a short, perky eighth-grade girl kissed her ninth-grade girlfriend of one year. I asked them where they met. "In church," they told me. Not far from them, a 14-year-old named Misti—who came out to classmates at her middle school when she was 12 and weathered anti-gay harassment and bullying, including having food thrown at her in the cafeteria—sat on a wooden bench and cuddled with a new girlfriend.

Austin had practically forgotten about his boyfriend. Instead, he was confessing to me—mostly by text message, though we were standing next to each other—his crush on Laddie, a 16-year-old who had just moved to Tulsa from a small town in Texas. Like Austin, Laddie was attending the dance for the first time, but he came off as much more comfortable in his skin and had a handful of admirers on the patio. Laddie told them that he came out in eighth grade and that the announcement sent shock waves through his Texas school.

"I definitely lost some friends," he said, "but no one really made fun of me or called me names, probably because I was one of the most popular kids when I came out. I don't think I would have come out if I wasn't popular."

"When I first realized I was gay," Austin interjected, "I just assumed I would hide it and be miserable for the rest of my life. But then I said, 'O.K., wait, I don't want to hide this and be miserable my whole life.'"

I asked him how old he was when he made that decision.

"Eleven," he said.

As the dance wound down and the boys waited for their rides home, I joined Tim Gillean, one of Openarms's founders, in the DJ booth, where he was preparing to play the Rihanna song "Disturbia." An affable 52-year-old with wire-rimmed glasses and salt-and-pepper hair, he founded Openarms in 2002 with his longtime partner, Ken Draper. In addition to the weekly dances, the couple lead discussion groups every Thursday—about self-esteem, healthy relationships and HIV/AIDS.

When I asked Gillean if he ever expected kids as young as Nick and Austin to show up at Openarms, he chuckled and shook his head. Like many adult gay men who came out in college or later, Gillean couldn't imagine openly gay middle school students. "But here they are," he said, looking out over the crowd. "More and more of them every week."

For many gay youth, middle school is more survival than learning.

Schools Aren't Prepared

I heard similar accounts from those who work with gay youth all across the country. Though most adolescents who come out do so in high school, sex researchers and counselors say that middle school students are increasingly coming out to friends or family or to an adult in school. Just how they're faring in a world that wasn't expecting them—and that isn't so sure a 12-year-old can know if he's gay—is a complicated question that defies simple geographical explanations. Though gay kids in the South and in rural areas tend to have a harder time than those on the coasts, I met gay youth who were doing well in socially conservative areas like Tulsa and others in progressive cities who were afraid to come out.

What is clear is that for many gay youth, middle school is more survival than learning—one parent of a gay teenager I spent time with likened her child's middle school to a "war zone." In a 2007 survey of 626 gay, bisexual and transgender middle schoolers from across the country by the Gay, Lesbian and Straight Education Network (GLSEN), 81 percent reported being regularly harassed on campus because of their sexual orientation. Another 39 percent reported physical assaults. Of the students who told teachers or administrators about the bullying, only 29 percent said it resulted in effective intervention.

A middle school counselor in Maine summed up the view of many educators I spoke to when she conceded that her school was "totally unprepared" for openly gay students. "We always knew middle school was a time when kids struggle with their identity," she told me, "but it was easy to let anti-gay language slide because it's so embedded in middle school culture and because we didn't have students who were out to us or their classmates. Now we do, so we're playing catch up to try to keep them safe."

Something needs to be done to curb anti-gay bullying.

As a response to anti-gay bullying and harassment, at least 120 middle schools across the country have formed gay-straight alliance (GSA) groups, where gay and lesbian students—and their straight peers—meet to brainstorm strategies for making their campuses safer. Other schools are letting students be part of the national Day of Silence each April (participants take a vow of silence for a day to symbolize the silencing effect of anti-gay harassment), which last year [2008] was held in memory of Lawrence King, a 15-year-old gay junior high student in Oxnard, Calif., who was shot and killed at school by a 14-year-old classmate.

Both GSAs and the Day of Silence have been controversial in places, as some parents and faculty members object to what they see as the promotion of homosexuality in public schools and the "premature sexualization of the students," as a lawyer for a school in central Florida that was fighting the creation of a GSA put it. But there is a growing consensus among parents and middle school educators that something needs to be done to curb anti-gay bullying, which a 2008 study at an all-male school by researchers at the University of Nebraska and Harvard Medical School found to be the most psychologically harmful type of bullying.

"I certainly don't believe school districts should force a sexual agenda on the community," says Finn Laursen, the executive director of the Christian Educators Association International, "but we can't just put our heads in the sand and ignore the kind of harassment that's going on."

Being young and gay is no longer an automatic prescription for a traumatic childhood.

The challenging school experience of so many gay and lesbian students—and the suicides last spring of a sixth grader in Massachusetts and a fifth grader in Georgia, both of whom were relentlessly bullied at school for appearing gay—reinforces the longtime narrative of gay youth in crisis. Studies in the '80s and '90s found gay teenagers to be at a significantly higher risk for depression, substance abuse and suicide than their heterosexual peers.

The New Gay Adolescent Is Proud and Resilient

When I went to work in 1998 for *XY*, a national magazine for young gay men, we received dozens of letters each week from teenagers in the depths of despair. Some had been thrown out by their families; others lived at home, but were reminded often that they were intrinsically flawed. My arrival at *XY* (at 23, I was only three years out of the closet myself) coincided with the founding of the Trevor Project, which runs a national 24-hour crisis and suicide hotline for gay and questioning youth, and with the first large wave of GSAs in high schools. (They are now in more than 4,000 high schools, according to GLSEN.)

But by the time I stopped writing for the magazine nearly three years later, the content of the letters we received was beginning to change. A new kind of gay adolescent was appearing on the page—proud, resilient, sometimes even happy. We profiled many of them in the magazine, including a seventh grader in suburban Philadelphia who was out to his classmates and a high school varsity football player from Massachusetts who came out to his teammates and was shocked to find unconditional support.

That's not to say that gay teenagers didn't still suffer harassment at school or rejection at home, but many seemed less burdened with shame and self-loathing than their older gay peers. What had changed? Not only were there increasingly accurate and positive portrayals of gays and lesbians in popular culture, but most teenagers were by then regular Internet users. Going online broke through the isolation that had been a hallmark of being young and gay, and it allowed gay teenagers to find information to refute what their families or churches sometimes still told them—namely, that they would never find happiness and love.

Today, nearly a decade after my time at *XY*, young people with same-sex attractions are increasingly coming out and living lives that would be "nearly incomprehensible to earlier generations of gay youth," Ritch Savin-Williams writes in his book *The New Gay Teenager*. A professor of developmental psychology at Cornell University, Savin-Williams told me recently that being young and gay is no longer an automatic prescription for a traumatic childhood.

In particular, openly gay youth who are perceived as conforming to adolescent gender norms are often fully integrated into their peer and school social circles. Girls who come out as bisexual, but are still considered "feminine" are often immune from harassment, as are some gay boys, like Laddie, who come out but are still considered "masculine." "Bisexual girls have it the easiest," Austin told me in Oklahoma. "Most of the straight guys at school think that's hot, so that can make the girl even more popular."

Still, the younger they are when they come out, the more that youth with same-sex attractions face an obstacle that would be unimaginable to their straight peers. When a 12-year-old boy matter-of-factly tells his parents—or a school counselor—that he likes girls, their reaction tends not to be one of disbelief, dismissal or rejection. "No one says to them: 'Are you sure? You're too young to know if you like girls. It's probably just a phase,'" says Eileen Ross, the director of the Outlet Program, a support service for gay youth in Mountain View, Calif. "But that's what we say too often to gay youth. We deny them their feelings and truth in a way we would never do with a heterosexual young person." . . .

It Can Be Cool to Be Open-Minded

On the national Day of Silence last April, I visited Daniel Webster Middle School in Los Angeles, one of 21 middle schools in California with a GSA. California is one of only 12 states that have passed laws to protect students from bullying and harassment on the basis of sexual orientation and gender identity or expression. (In May, Representative Linda Sánchez of California introduced the Safe Schools Improvement Act, a federal anti-bullying bill that would require schools to implement comprehensive anti-bullying policies that include protections for gay students.)

I arrived at Daniel Webster, a school of some 850 students, most of them Hispanic or African American, at lunchtime. About 50 kids milled around two large wooden tables at the center of the school's leafy courtyard. Many of them wore pink T-shirts, and some filled out cards that would later be strung together and displayed: "You Are What You Are—Embrace It," "Never Put Someone Down, and Never Let Someone Put You Down." Others communicated using hand gestures or by writing notes to one another. But most had given up trying to be mute. "Good luck getting middle schoolers not to talk," the school's counselor and GSA co-adviser at the time, Ruben Valerio, told me with a smile.

One of the loudest students at the tables was Johnny (a nickname), a tall, handsome seventh grader. A leader of the GSA, he had only managed to stay quiet for about 30 seconds that morning. "It's just really exciting to be at a school where it's O.K. to be gay," he told me as he bear-hugged his friend, an outgoing seventh grader known to her friends as Lala, who'd come out earlier that year as bisexual. At his previous school, Johnny didn't feel safe and had little support when he came out to his mother. "She would go back and forth between saying things like: 'I love you. I just don't understand why you would choose this lifestyle at this age,' to 'It's disgusting what you're doing. Are you a faggot now?' No one would ever use that word here."

Johnny estimated that there were about 35 girls and 10 boys at Daniel Webster who were out as bisexual, lesbian or gay. (The vast majority of those girls identified as bisexual.) He introduced me to a handful of them, including two members of the GSA: Tina (also a nickname), a seventh grader who considered herself bisexual and was dating a boy at another school; and a popular eighth-grade girl who used to date Tina.

They were joined at the tables by dozens of their straight friends and a handful of teachers. One teacher, Richard Mandl, approached me and asked what I thought of the school. I told him that I'd never seen so many happy gay kids in one place. "It's a little disorienting," I told him. "I feel like I'm in a parallel gay universe."

He laughed. "Yeah, it's pretty unusual what's happened here," he said. "It definitely wasn't always this way."

When Mandl began teaching at the school in 2002, he said that there weren't any openly gay students—and that it was common to hear anti-gay language. "Kids would run by you and be screaming at another kid: 'You fag! You're so gay!'" he said. "It wasn't until a few years ago when the faculty sort of came together and said: 'You know what? We need to stop this.'"

That became a lot easier two years ago when one of the school's most popular boys came out to his classmates. Because he was so well liked, and because so many of his friends rallied around him, "it became cooler at Daniel Webster to be accepting and open-minded," Mandl said.

Not all principals have reacted as enthusiastically to students or teachers hoping to start a GSA [gay-straight alliance].

The principal, Kendra Wallace, told me that she didn't hesitate when the school's science teacher approached her (on behalf of the boy and several of his friends) about starting a GSA. "I had some staff who were livid at first, because they thought it would be about sex, or us endorsing a lifestyle," she said. "But the GSA isn't about that, and they've come around. This is a club that promotes safety, and it gives kids a voice.

And the most amazing thing has happened since the GSA started. Bullying of all kinds is way down. The GSA created this pervasive anti-bullying culture on campus that affects everyone."

The Controversy over Gay-Straight Alliance Groups

Not all principals have reacted as enthusiastically to students or teachers hoping to start a GSA. (Teachers often wait for students to make the request, because they don't want to be perceived as "having a political agenda," as one school counselor told me.) At a middle school in Massachusetts, the GSA adviser told me that the school's principal initially balked when students asked to observe the Day of Silence and start a GSA. "She argued that it wasn't age-appropriate, and she worried about having to deal with negative editorials in the local paper," the adviser said. But because the school had other extracurricular clubs, "the principal was made aware that blocking a GSA from forming is against the law."

Indeed, courts—citing the Equal Access Act, which requires public schools to provide equal access to extracurricular clubs—have consistently ruled against schools that try to block GSAs from starting. (The 1984 law was the brainchild of Christian groups fighting to allow students to form religious clubs in schools.)

When Yulee High School in northeast Florida was forced by a federal judge last spring to let a GSA meet on campus, the school asked students to change the name of their proposed club to something other than Gay-Straight Alliance. The students refused, and a court backed them up in August. Administrators at Austin's middle school in Michigan used the same tactic when he tried to start a GSA there, he said. "They told me I needed to change the name to something 'less controversial,'" Austin recalled. "I didn't feel like fighting them, so I just called it the Peace Alliance."

And because there were so few openly gay students at Austin's middle school last year, all but two of the 15 or so students who attended each meeting were straight. At GSA meetings at Daniel Webster, gay and straight members spend two periods a week reading and discussing news stories about gay issues, organizing events like the Day of Silence and talking about navigating the outside world—which isn't always as supportive as their campus. Lala, for example, said the backing of the GSA was critical when she came out to her family.

"They're a lot better now, but the first thing one of my relatives did when I told them I was bisexual was hit me on the head with a Bible," she told me. "So while I was dealing with that insanity at home, I at least had a safe place at school to talk about what was happening."

14

Teens Are Not as Sexually Promiscuous as Adults Fear

Cathy Young

Cathy Young is a contributing editor for Reason *magazine and a columnist for the* Boston Globe. *She has written two books:* Growing Up in Moscow: Memories of a Soviet Girlhood *and* Ceasefire!: Why Women and Men Must Join Forces to Achieve True Equality.

Headlines about a teenage oral sex craze in the late 1990s kept parents on edge. Stories circulated about middle school orgies at which teen girls took turns servicing their male counterparts; even Oprah Winfrey voiced her alarm. These stories were surely exaggerated. In fact, statistically, oral sex has not really increased among teens. While it may be disturbing that some kids are having sex too soon and with too many partners, the teen oral sex craze is a myth. Parents and teens alike will be better served by focusing more on the real problems of growing up.

I s oral sex really the latest teen craze?

The teenage oral sex panic began in the late 1990s. It is in some ways a part of the [former president Bill] Clinton legacy—more specifically, the Clinton-[Monica] Lewinsky legacy. It was Clinton's most famous line ("I did not have sexual relations with that woman, Miss Lewinsky") and the subsequent debate on whether receiving oral sex qualified as

Cathy Young, "The Great Fellatio Scare," *Reason*, May 2006, vol. 38, no. 1, pp. 18–20. Copyright © 2006 by Reason Foundation, 3415 S. Sepulveda Blvd., Suite 400, Los Angeles, CA 90034, www.reason.com. Reproduced by permission.

"sexual relations" that produced the apparently shocking disclosure that a lot of teenagers were not only engaging in oral sex, but regarding it as not quite sex.

Worse: According to press accounts, America's young Monicas weren't just having oral sex; they were having it in circumstances that would raise [*Playboy* publisher] Hugh Hefner's eyebrows. In July 1998, the *Washington Post* ran a front-page story with the headline, "Parents Are Alarmed by an Unsettling New Fad in Middle Schools: Oral Sex."

Its main example was a scandal in an Arlington, Virginia, school, where a group of eighth graders would get together for parties at which boys and girls paired off for sexual activities that eventually progressed from petting to oral sex. There were also a couple reported instances of public fellatio, on a school bus and in a hallway, that reached school authorities "through the student grapevine."

Feminists saw girls as victims of male dominance, while conservatives blamed feminists.

From here, it was only a short step to tales of "rainbow parties" where several girls wearing different colors of lipstick would take turns servicing a boy until their lipstick traces formed a "rainbow" of rings. In 2003, this peril was explored by Oprah [Winfrey] herself, with the help of *O: The Oprah Magazine* feature writer Michelle Burford, who interviewed 50 girls, some as young as nine, and painted a frightening picture of kiddie debauchery. "Are rainbow parties pretty common?" inquired a rapt Oprah, to which Burford replied, "I think so. At least among the 50 girls that I talked to . . . this was pervasive."

Burford did not say whether the girls had told her they themselves had attended such parties, or if they had simply heard rumors. Nor was any proof produced of what was actually said in those interviews.

All these stories invariably depicted the oral sex as almost entirely one-sided, with girls giving and boys receiving. "One more opportunity for male satisfaction and female degradation in the name of adolescent sexual curiosity," harrumphed *Baltimore Sun* columnist Susan Reimer. In this familiar script, feminists saw girls as victims of male dominance, while conservatives blamed feminists and Clinton, whose bad example supposedly sent kids the message that fellatio was OK.

Now the "rainbow party" tale—which has never been substantiated and may well have originated with that *Washington Post* story—has become the subject of a novel, Paul Ruditis's *The Rainbow Party*, published last summer [2005] by Simon Pulse, a young adult division of Simon & Schuster. While conservatives have widely denounced the book as yet another excrescence of our licentious culture, its message actually seems to be one of almost old-fashioned moralism: The girl who plans the party is humiliated when hardly anyone shows up, then punished with a gonorrhea infection to boot.

Ruditis's novel has prompted a new round of hand wringing. On the Fox News Channel's *Hannity & Colmes*, radio psychologist Judy Kuriansky asserted that teenagers had been telling her about rainbow parties for years on her show, and assured the shocked hosts that yes, those parties really were going on. "Unbelievable," sputtered Sean Hannity.

Oral Sex Has Not Really Increased Among Teens

Unbelievable, indeed. For one, as Caitlin Flanagan points out in a lengthy review essay in the *Atlantic*, the different colors of lipstick would almost inevitably smear and destroy the supposedly sought-after rainbow effect. Besides, a boy would have to be a sexual super-athlete to complete the circuit. The "current oral sex hysteria," Flanagan writes, "requires believing that a boy could be serviced at the school bus–train party—receiving oral sex from ten or fifteen girls, one after another—and then zip his fly and head off to homeroom, first stopping in the stairwell for a quickie to tide him over until math."

Unfortunately, while Flanagan—who has recently drawn attention with her tart, often thoughtful critiques of feminism—starts on a skeptical note, she turns around about a third of the way into her sprawling, nearly 9,000-word tract and succumbs to the hysteria. She dismisses the tales of orgies and rampant anonymous blow jobs as nonsense, noting that she has been able to find only one verified account of a girl performing oral sex on multiple boys at a party. Yet she thinks the reality is bad enough.

"We've made a world for our girls in which the pornography industry has become increasingly mainstream," Flanagan writes, "in which Planned Parenthood's response to the oral sex craze has been to set up a help line, in which the forces of feminism have worked relentlessly to erode the patriarchy— which, despite its manifold evils, held that providing for the sexual safety of young girls was among its primary reasons for existence. And here are America's girls: experienced beyond their years, lacking any clear message from the adult community about the importance of protecting their modesty, adrift in one of the most explicitly sexualized cultures in the history of the world. Here are America's girls: on their knees."

What is the basis for this Wendy Shalit-style outburst? [Shalit is a conservative author who advocates modest dress.] A study by the National Center for Health Statistics and the Centers for Disease Control and Prevention, released in September 2005, found that 25 percent of 15-year-old girls and half of 17-year-olds had engaged in oral sex. While the survey did not include children under 15, the report noted that in a survey several months earlier, only 4 percent of adolescents 13 to 14 years old said they'd had oral sex. (Did any of this represent an increase from the past? Probably not: A Child Trends' analysis of data from surveys of unmarried males ages 15 to 19 in 1995 and 2002 found no significant changes in reported rates of oral sex experience.)

While Flanagan talks about sex "outside of romantic relationships," the September 2005 study said nothing about the context in which these activities took place—casual encounters or steady dating.

The study did say something about one aspect of the alleged oral sex craze, something that contradicts conventional wisdom. Girls and boys, it turns out, are about equally likely to give and to receive. Actually, at least among younger adolescents, boys overall reported more oral sex experience than girls, but both boys and girls were more likely to report receiving oral sex than giving it—which suggests a lot of respondents are fibbing.

The majority [of teens] do not inhabit the sexual jungle of worried adults' imaginations.

This finding was so counterintuitive that some "experts" chose to disbelieve it: Joe McIlhaney Jr., chairman of the Medical Institute for Sexual Health, told the *Washington Post* he doubted that girls were really enjoying oral sex: "I'd like to know a whole lot more about the pressure boys put on girls." Others, such as James Wagoner of the reproductive health organization Advocates for Youth, argued that the new data subverted the stereotype of boys as predators and girls as prey.

How does Flanagan deal with this information? By refusing to deal with it. Throughout the article, she assumes girls are only the givers, referring to "this strange new preference for unreciprocated oral sex" and even speculating that girls, ill-served by our modesty-unfriendly culture, have taken to giving oral sex in order to keep their own sexuality protected from male encroachments. (Boys, Flanagan adds, aren't vulnerable to the emotional repercussions of sex the way girls are, so as a mother of boys she has little personal concern about the oral peril.)

Are some kids having sex too soon, and with too many partners, for their own emotional and physical well-being? Almost certainly. But the majority do not inhabit the sexual jungle of worried adults' imaginations. The teenage fellatio craze exists mainly among adults. To those in the audience who are not worried parents, it provides both sexual and moralistic thrills; it plays both to the prurient fascination with teenage girls gone wild and to the paternalistic stereotype of girls as victims. It does very little to help either adolescents or their parents deal with the real problems of growing up.

Organizations to Contact

The editors have compiled the following list of organizations concerned with the issues debated in this book. The descriptions are derived from materials provided by the organizations. All have publications or information available for interested readers. The list was compiled on the date of publication of the present volume; names, addresses, phone and fax numbers, and e-mail and Internet addresses may change. Be aware that many organizations take several weeks or longer to respond to inquiries, so allow as much time as possible.

About-Face
PO Box 77665, San Francisco, CA   94107
(415) 436-0212
e-mail: info@about-face.org
Web site: www.about-face.org

About-Face is an organization working to educate women and young girls about harmful media portrayals and images of women and how to resist these influences. It does this through three primary programs: Education into Action media literacy workshops, Take Action, and their Web site, About-Face.org. Included in the information available on the Web site are examples of what the group believes are the worst offenders of sexualization of women and girls in the media.

Campaign for a Commercial-Free Childhood (CCFC)
89 South Street, Suite 404, Boston, MA   02111
(857) 241-2028 • fax: (617) 737-1585
e-mail: ccfc@commercialfreechildhood.org
Web site: www.commercialexploitation.org

Founded in 2000, Campaign for a Commercial-Free Childhood (CCFC) has taken on some of the largest corporations in the world in an attempt to take back childhood from corporate marketing. Made up of parents, educators, health care professionals and others, it is a national organization devoted to limiting commercial culture's influence on children. Its Web site features fact sheets, articles, and publications, including *CCFC Guide to Commercial-Free Holidays 2009*, to help parents find strategies for raising healthy children in a commercialized culture.

Center on Media and Child Health (CMCH)

300 Longwood Avenue, Boston, MA 02115
(617) 355-2000
e-mail: cmch@childrens.harvard.edu
Web site: www.cmch.tv

Based at Children's Hospital Boston, Harvard Medical School, and Harvard School of Public Health, the Center on Media and Child Health (CMCH) conducts and compiles research to improve the understanding of the ways in which media affects children. It lends its expertise to programs that address children's exposure to the media. Current news articles as well as up-to-date information are available on its Web site.

Coalition for Positive Sexuality (CPS)

PO Box 77212, Washington, DC 20013
(773) 604-1654
Web site: www.positive.org

The Coalition for Positive Sexuality (CPS) began in 1996 as a poster project geared toward girls, encouraging them to acknowledge their sexuality, not deny it. The coalition aims to give teens the information they need to make informed decisions regarding sex and sexuality and creates an open dialogue through which teens learn the importance of safe sex through condom use. The coalition's current publication, *Just Say Yes*, can be obtained by visiting its Web site.

Free Child Project

PO Box 6185, Olympia, WA 98507
(360) 489-9680

e-mail: info@freechild.org
Web site: www.freechild.org

The Free Child Project's mission is to get teens active in social change, especially when it affects them most. The group works to fight adultism, sexism, heterosexism, and social hierarchies as well as many other forms of injustice against youth.

Media Awareness Network (MNet)

950 Gladstone Avenue, Suite 120, Ottowa, Ontario   K1Y 3E6 Canada

(613) 224-7721 • fax: (613) 224-1958

e-mail: info@media-awareness.ca

Web site: www.media-awareness.ca

Since its beginning in 1996, the Media Awareness Network (MNet) has incorporated into its team educators, journalists, and people with backgrounds in mass communication and cultural policy. Its goal is to provide youth with the education needed to understand how the media works and how it affects them and the choices they make. The Web site offers separate resources for teachers and parents as well as a blog and news on current issues regarding the media.

Scarleteen

1752 NW Market Street, No. 627, Seattle, WA   98107

Web site: www.scarleteen.com

In 1998, Heather Corinna and several volunteers created Scarleteen when, via a separate Web site, e-mails began coming in from the younger population asking different questions about sex, making it obvious that there was a need for a sex education site for teens. With its content being used by several major organizations, including Planned Parenthood and UNICEF (the United Nations Children's Fund), Scarleteen provides answers to questions about sex and sexuality that teens may be too embarrassed to talk about with their parents or teachers.

Sexuality Information and Education Council of the United States (SIECUS)

90 John Street, Suite 704, New York, NY 10038
(212) 819-9770 • fax: (212) 819-9776
e-mail: pmalone@siecus.org
Web site: www.siecus.org

The Sexuality Information and Education Council of the United States (SIECUS) was founded in 1964 by Dr. Mary Calderone as a result of her concern for the lack of information available for young people as well as adults on sex and sexuality. SIECUS provides a place where sexuality is viewed as natural and healthy. Since its beginning, SIECUS has taken a stand on major issues concerning sexuality, including the role of sexuality in society and culture. Its Web site features many publications, including *Guidelines for Comprehensive Sexuality Education* and *Filling the Gaps: Hard-to-Teach Topics in Sexuality Education.*

TakingITGlobal

33 Flatbush Avenue, Brooklyn, NY 11217
(212) 661-6111 • fax: (212) 661-1933
e-mail: info@takingitglobal.org
Web site: www.tigweb.org

TakingITGlobal was started in 1999 by Jennifer Corriero and Michael Furdyk with the goal of encouraging youth to cooperate together in making the world a better place. Providing tools that give youth access to global opportunities and connections, TakingITGlobal motivates teens to take responsibility for improving their social environment. The Web site offers information for youth activities as well as information for educators and other organizations looking for ideas on how to get teens involved.

Youth Incentives

PO Box 9022, Utrecht 3506 GA
    The Netherlands
31 (0)30 2332322 • fax: 31 (0)30 2319387

e-mail: info@youthincentives.org
Web site: www.youthincentives.org

Youth Incentives was developed by Rutgers Nisso Groep, an expert center on sexuality, located in the Netherlands. Its approach to lowering teen pregnancy and sexually transmitted diseases is through education and openness about the sexuality of youth. Youth Incentives' goal is to ensure all young people enjoy the safety, confidence, and pleasure that goes along with relationships and safe sex by encouraging teens to make informed decisions regarding sex and their reproductive health.

Bibliography

Books

Sharlene Azam   *Oral Sex Is the New Goodnight Kiss:*
                     The Sexual Bullying of Girls. India:
                     Bollywood Filmed Entertainment
                     Inc., 2008.

Audrey D.   *All Made Up: A Girl's Guide to Seeing*
Brashich   *Through Celebrity Hype to Celebrate*
                     Real Beauty. New York: Walker &
                     Co., 2006.

M. Gigi Durham   *The Lolita Effect: The Media*
                     Sexualization of Young Girls and
                     What We Can Do About It. New
                     York: Overlook Press, 2008.

Michael Kimmel   *Guyland: The Perilous World Where*
                     Boys Become Men. New York:
                     HarperCollins Publishers, 2008.

Sharon Lamb and   *Packaging Girlhood: Rescuing Our*
Lyn Mikel Brown   *Daughters from Marketers' Schemes.*
                     New York: St. Martin's Press, 2006.

Diane E. Levin   *So Sexy So Soon: The New Sexualized*
and Jean   *Childhood and What Parents Can Do*
Kilbourne   *to Protect Their Kids.* New York:
                     Ballantine Books, 2008.

Carol Platt Liebau   *Prude: How the Sex-Obsessed Culture*
                     Damages Girls (and America, Too!).
                     New York: Center Street, 2007.

Sharna Olfman, ed.	*Childhood Lost: How American Culture Is Failing Our Kids.* Westport, CT: Praeger Publishers, 2005.
Sharna Olfman, ed.	*The Sexualization of Childhood.* Westport, CT: Praeger Publishers, 2009.
Patrice A. Oppliger	*Girls Gone Skank: The Sexualization of Girls in American Culture.* Jefferson, NC: McFarland & Company, 2008.
C.J. Pascoe	*Dude, You're a Fag: Masculinity and Sexuality in High School.* Berkeley, CA: University of California Press, 2007.
T. Denean Sharpley-Whiting	*Pimps Up, Ho's Down: Hip Hop's Hold on Young Black Women.* New York: New York University Press, 2007.

Periodicals

Anne Marie Aikin	"Playing Dress-Up," *Alive*, September 2008.
Rosa Brooks	"No Escaping Sexualization of Young Girls," *Los Angeles Times*, August 25, 2006.
Mona Charen	"Sexualizing Girls," *National Review Online*, February 23, 2007. www.nationalreview.com.
Susan J. Douglas	"The Jamie Lynn Effect," *In These Times*, January 22, 2008.

R. Danielle Egan and Gail L. Hawkes — "Endangered Girls and Incendiary Objects: Unpacking the Discourse on Sexualization," *Sexuality & Culture*, December 2008.

Kerry Howley — "Invasion of the Prostitots: Another Moral Panic About American Girls," *Reason*, July 1, 2007.

Kari Lerum and Shari L. Dworkin — "Toward an Interdisciplinary Dialogue on Youth, Sexualization, and Health," *Journal of Sex Research*, July 2009.

Belinda Luscombe — "The Truth About Teen Girls," *Time*, September 11, 2008.

Susan B. McConnell — "The Sexualization of Girls," SusanBMcConnell.com, September 30, 2009. http://susanbmcconnell.com.

Trina Read — "Are Today's Teens Hyper-Sexual (or Are Parents Just Prudes)?" *National Post*, June 24, 2009.

Lindor Reynolds — "Public's Apathy Enables Sexualization of Children," *Winnipeg Free Press*, May 14, 2009.

Joanne Richard — "Selling Sex to Kids," *Toronto Sun*, July 17, 2005.

Bradford G. Schleifer — "Innocence Lost—The Sexualization of Youth," *Real Truth*, December 10, 2007.

Brigid Schulte	"Preteens Trading Fairy Wands for Fishnets," *Washington Post*, October 30, 2007.
Ine Vanwesenbeeck	"The Risks and Rights of Sexualization: An Appreciative Commentary on Lerum and Dworkin's 'Bad Girls Rule,'" *Journal of Sex Research*, July 2009.
Judith Warner	"Hot Tots, and Moms Hot to Trot (Sexualization of Children)," *New York Times*, March 17, 2007.
Stacy Weiner	"Goodbye to Girlhood," *Washington Post*, February 20, 2007.
Eileen Zurbriggen	"Message and the Media: Our Girls Deserve Better," *San Francisco Chronicle*, February 26, 2007.

Index

A

Abortion rates, 38
AboutKidsHealth, 10–17
Abstinence-based programs, 26
Abuse. *See* Rape; Sexual abuse
Acquaintance rape, 18, 19
Actresses. *See* Celebrities
Advertising. *See* Media
Age issues
    lowering adulthood, 30
    sexual exploitation, 52
    tweens, early defining, 13, 58
Aggression, physical, 31–35
    See also Sexual abuse; Sexual violence
Aggression, social. *See* Bullying; Sexual harassment
Alcohol and drugs
    abuse and rehab, celebrities, 39, 65
    rape and, 19, 44
    sexual exploitation media, 52
American Girl dolls, 37
American Pregnancy Association, 7
American Psychological Association
    report, dangers/harms of sexualization, 11–12, 18, 41–42, 45, 52
    reports criticized, 36, 37–40
Animated movies, 10, 12, 37
Anorexia nervosa, 16
Athletes, professional
    men, 21, 33
    women, 12
    See also Sports participation
Attractiveness
    popularity component, 13, 14
    sexiness valued above all, 15, 19, 23, 45, 46, 52, 59, 69, 70, 71–73
    See also Idealized beauty

B

Beauty pageants, 11, 27, 42
Beauty standards. *See* Attractiveness; Idealized beauty
Behavior. *See* Eroticised behavior in children; Sexual activity
Bell, Rachel, 18–21
Best Friends program, 26–27
Biel, Jessica, 67–68
Bisexuality, 80, 86, 87–88
Body image
    conformity, 13, 15, 69, 72
    mental functioning and, 15
    negative, sexualization's effects, 10, 13, 14, 16, 19, 45
Boys and men
    physical aggression and encouragement as sexualization, 31–35
    sexual desire and activity, expectations and acceptance, 7, 8, 44–45
    sexualization, and abuse of girls/women, 7–8, 13–14, 18–21, 73
    sexualization harms development, 11, 21, 69, 73
    struggles, achievement, 24, 39

D

D'Agostino, Joseph A., 41–46

Dancing
children's eroticised behavior,
28–29, 30, 32
pole-, 27, 70

Daniel Webster Middle School
(Los Angeles), 86–88, 90

Dating violence, 8, 19

Day of Silence, 83–84, 89, 90

Denizet-Lewis, Benoit, 79–90

Depression, 16, 19, 36, 38, 39, 45,
52, 58

Diaries, 45, 46

Dieting, 16

*Dilemmas of Desire: Teenage Girls
Talk About Sexuality* (Tolman),
7–8

Disney movies, 10, 12, 37

Disney stars, 60, 61, 63, 65, 68

"Do-me feminism," 24–25, 41

Dolls, 8, 13, 37, 38, 39, 42, 58

Domesticity, 41, 42, 45–46

Downes, Lawrence, 28–30, 31, 32–
33, 34–35

Drug use. *See* Alcohol and drugs

Durham, M. Gigi, 69–78

E

Eating disorders, 16, 38, 45, 52, 58

Education
media literacy, 10, 17, 77
sex, 17, 70, 73, 75, 76, 77

Empowerment, via sex, 24–25

Equal Access Act (1984), 89

Eroticised behavior in children,
11, 28–30, 31, 32, 42

Exploitation. *See* Sexual exploitation

F

Family dialogues, 10, 17, 69, 76–
77, 78
See also Parents

Fashion
industry fashion shows, 11, 42
thinness ideals, 16
trends and marketing, provocative clothing, 8, 11, 13,
37–38, 42, 52, 55, 58, 59, 61,
69, 70, 71

Fathers
influences, daughters, 13, 17
should not exploit daughters'
sexuality, 60–63
See also Parents

Femininity
gender norms, gay/bisexual
girls, 86
narrow definitions, 8–9, 56,
71–72, 75

Feminism
"do-me" feminism, 24–25, 41
domesticity devaluing, 41, 42,
45–46
feminist critiques, corporate
media sexualization, 69–78
feminist men, as objectifiers,
41, 42–44
feminists to blame for sexualization of girls, 41–46

Flanagan, Caitlin, 93–94, 95

Football, 31, 33–34

Forced sexual intercourse. *See*
Rape

Free Speech Coalition, 53